D0707887

HOME SERVICE BOOK

by
JOAN STOREY

Author of
"Concise Basic Cookery"

JOAN STOREY'S
HOME SERVICE BOOK

The answers to your everyday problems in the home

With numerous line drawings
by Nora L. Southworth
and
67 half-tone illustrations

LONDON

HODDER AND STOUGHTON

First Printed 1955

MADE AND PRINTED IN GREAT BRITAIN FOR
HODDER AND STOUGHTON LIMITED, LONDON
BY C. TINLING & CO. LTD., LIVERPOOL, LONDON
AND PRESCOT

CONTENTS

LIST OF ILLUSTRATIONS

LIST OF ILLUSTRATIONS

Plates 13–24
between pages 80–81

THE HOME SERVICE BOOK

You will find in this book the answers to many of the problems that I am being asked almost every day through my Home Service Centres in the big shops all over the country and through my editorial Home Service in *Housewife* magazine. They are the sort of problems which have always existed, but until now have frequently gone unanswered because people had no idea where to go to find the answers.

I believe that the information will enable the housewife and her husband to avoid mistakes when setting up home and buying new domestic equipment, furniture and upholstery. It will also enable them to maintain the home in the most efficient and economical manner and get the best service from the things that they have got.

A special feature of my work is that I am completely free of manufacturer's influence. The Home Service Centres are sponsored by the important independent shops all over the country and in the case of *Housewife*, by that magazine. This enables me to give completely genuine unbiased advice and where I believe it will help the reader, to mention the name of the product which is particularly suited to a special purpose.

The fact that only a very small number of products are mentioned in the book does in no way indicate that I do not approve of other products of the same type; to mention all the good products of which I approve would fill several books. Readers who are in doubt can consult my trained experts at my Home Service Centres; advice is, of course, entirely free.

Products are recommended only after exhaustive technical and practical tests conducted by top-rank experts in the various fields; I personally test the products in my home to discover the sort of reactions a housewife is likely to experience.

I am grateful for the whole-hearted support of manufacturers, and associations connected with manufacturers, as well as nationally sponsored technical organisations, which has made this work possible, and enabled me to offer information and advice based on the highest authority available.

JOAN STOREY

April, 1955

HOUSEHOLD PROBLEMS

The enamel on my new cooker is badly chipped on two corners and more enamel keeps on flaking off. Is there anything I can do?

Use a very smooth paste of "Alabastine" to level up the chipped surface, then when quite dry, rub this with very fine glass paper and brush with a paint of exactly the same shade as the cooker; the chipped corners should then be unnoticeable.

I notice a crack in our otherwise perfectly good lavatory basin. Is there any way I can stop it spreading?

Brush a good grade of white lead paint over the crack on the outside of the basin, allowing about $\frac{1}{2}$ inch of paint either side of the crack. Press a piece of strong muslin over the paint while it is still wet and leave to dry, then paint the muslin with the white lead and top with a narrower piece of muslin. When this is dry, paint this also, and leave till perfectly dry before using the basin.

This treatment may also be applied to cracked hand-basins but in both cases it is dangerous and unhygienic to use badly cracked basins.

Is there any way of making soap go further? Our family is particularly extravagant.

Soft soap lathers away more quickly than hard soap, so place your soap in the linen cupboard near the hot water storage tank to harden before use. This can serve a double purpose because if you choose a fragrantly scented soap it will impart a lovely faint perfume to your linen.

Do you advise soap or detergents for washing up?

Soapless detergents are good because they remove the grease easily, but they also remove the grease from the hands and make them rough and coarse unless a barrier cream is used or gloves are worn. The liquid detergents are useful because of their lack of lather, and soap powders give good results.

I am told that metal draining boards are liable to chip crockery unless one is very careful, and that I should be better off with a wooden board. Is this true?

No! Metal "gives" and is inclined to prevent chipping rather than cause it! I have used metal draining boards for years and cannot remember a time when the boards could be blamed for chipping crockery!

Recently I have had the misfortune to crack two of my glass ovenware dishes when they have come out of the oven. Could it be anything to do with the new plastic top that my husband has put on my kitchen table? Hot dishes cracked when they were put down on this table.

You have solved your own problem! The plastic type of surface, though excellent and labour saving, does not allow for contraction or expansion, and so when the hot glass ovenware is put down it is liable to crack. The solution is easy—put a cork or rubber mat on the table before putting down your hot dishes!

What is the best thing to do to stop the kitchen windows steaming over when the kitchen is steamy?

Rub over with a cloth dipped in a solution consisting of equal parts of glycerine and methylated spirits—this is equally good for car windscreens.

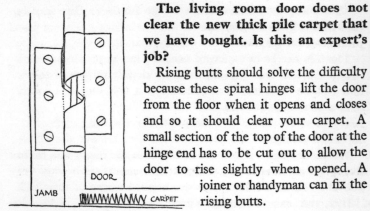

The living room door does not clear the new thick pile carpet that we have bought. Is this an expert's job?

Rising butts should solve the difficulty because these spiral hinges lift the door from the floor when it opens and closes and so it should clear your carpet. A small section of the top of the door at the hinge end has to be cut out to allow the door to rise slightly when opened. A joiner or handyman can fix the rising butts.

Is there a cure for rattling doors? I am beginning to lose hope!

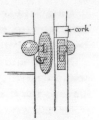

Cut a small piece of cork of the right thickness to make the door fit securely and glue this just above the lock then paint it the colour of the door—it works like a charm!

What is the best sort of covering for pantry shelves?

"Formica" or "Wareite" are ideal because they are so easy to keep clean and they can be fitted by the householder. But they are rather expensive for this purpose. Alternatives include linoleum, carefully laid to avoid gaps and crevices where spilt food and dirt can collect, plastic wall tiles such as the "Bex" and Stone and Simmons' tiles, which can be fitted by the handyman and are extremely easy to keep clean, and specially treated shelf paper like "Staynprufe" which can be sponged down.

The metal curtain runners make a very loud harsh noise when the curtains are drawn, and they often stick in their tracks.

Your curtain runners probably need oiling. A drop or two of oil should do the trick but be careful not to use too much or it may overflow and mark the curtains.

There are no picture rails in the house we are moving into and we are wondering how we can hang several good pictures that we have.

The "Patent Hook" picture hanger consists of a strong thin pin and a hook; the pin can be driven into a plaster wall and is so placed that it is driven in at a downward slanting angle and will hold quite heavy pictures safely. The hooks cost only a few coppers a packet.

We have been recommended to install Vita glass in our living room because it admits the sunshine; is this true and is it worth while?

It is true that Vita glass allows the passage of short-wave

ultra-violet rays, but in order for it to be fully effective the glass must be kept absolutely clean. Under these conditions, it is worth while, providing the room has a sunny aspect.

Do you know if there is any truth in the saying that yellow-tinted glass is good for a pantry window because it keeps the flies away?

Yes, this is true. There is an amber-tinted glass known as anti-fly glass, which is made for larder windows. Tests have proved that flies, like other insects, prefer a white to a coloured light, and red is the best deterrent. However, red glass involves too much loss of light, and so yellow is used and is said to be nearly as effective in discouraging flies.

TAPE BINDING

Is there any satisfactory method of lengthening the life of a perfectly good rough towel when the selvedges begin to tear?

Stitch a piece of tape round the edges.

My "rough" towels have worn thin and are no longer rough. Is there any way of putting more body into these towels?

Add a very little starch to the final rinsing water to give the towels the necessary body without stiffening them.

I have just bought a set of lovely enamel saucepans and want to know how to look after them.

Clean in soap and water, and avoid using abrasives of any sort. When food sticks to the insides of the pans leave them to soak for a time then use a nylon or soft pot brush or non-scratchy pot cleaner to remove the food. The greatest danger with enamel is chipping, so store them in a safe place where they cannot get knocked over or knocked against one another, accidentally.

Is there a way of seasoning a frying pan when the food is sticking badly?

Rub with a little grease and heat well. Remove from the heat, throw in a handful of salt and rub vigorously round the pan with a pad of newspaper. Rinse thoroughly before using the pan. Do not repeat often or the surface of the pan may be damaged.

Is there any way of removing obstinate tea stains from delicate china without using a brush which would possibly roughen the surface?

You are right not to use a stiff brush or even the mildest abrasive on china; you can usually remove tea stains by rubbing with a little borax or salt. A really soft brush is useful for removing marks from awkward crevices round the handle on the outside of the cup.

Have you any special tips for cleaning polythene bowls and other household articles made of this material? Can a household bleach be used without damaging the bowl?

Warm soapy water is all that is necessary to clean polythene; do not use for boiling clothes or place on a hot surface such as the top of the cooker or boiling ring. Polythene is unbreakable under normal conditions and unaffected by household chemicals, oils, fats and other household foodstuffs.

Is there any way of removing scratches from plastic articles? A cigarette box I have has some nasty surface scratches.

These sort of scratches can often be removed with a non-abrasive type of metal polish.

Are there any "baby" water softeners suitable for softening the water for toilet purposes, hair washing, etc.?

Yes, one of the first to be introduced was the Steralic "Master" which can be fitted on to the tap when you want it and is only a few inches long, and costs under £2.

My paying guests have a habit of leaving the taps of the bath dripping and I am scared of dark marks forming beneath the taps. Have you any suggestions?

One good way of bringing the matter to their notice and also of preventing the drips marking the bath would be to suspend small paste or sauce bottles on string beneath the taps for several days. Check the taps do not need new washers and are easy to turn off.

B

What is the best way to clear a blocked sink outlet?

Put a large handful of washing soda crystals over the sink outlet and pour down a kettleful of boiling water. This will remove any accumulated grease and very often clear the blockage. If it fails place a rubber force cup over the outlet and operate it with a vigorous up-and-down movement. If this fails, put a pail under the U-bend, unscrew the nut and remove any obstruction with piece of strong wire. Put some hot water down to flush away any remaining obstruction before replacing the nut and tightening it.

Our cold water taps have started to make rumbling noises when the taps are turned on. How can we stop this?

This is called "water hammer" and a new washer will often cure the trouble. But occasionally the water system is at fault and then the local water board are always pleased to come along and inspect the system; they seldom make a charge for this service.

I want to seal my wooden draining boards to prevent dirt and grease from penetrating, and eliminate scrubbing. How can I do it?

You need Bourne Seal which is quite inexpensive and easy to apply. It preserves the wood and saves a great deal of labour.

Two of my electric power plugs have worn loose in their sockets. What should I do?

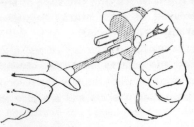

Slightly open the slit in each prong, using a screw-driver or other similar tool, and you will find the plugs will then fit firmly in their sockets.

What can I put on the walls round my sink? They are painted at present and look continually grubby. I am renting the house and therefore do not want to go to the expense of having the walls tiled.

The plastic wall tiles such as the "Bex" and Stone and Simmons, are inexpensive and you can fix them yourself providing the walls are level and smooth. Alternatively, you could fit panels of plastic board like "Formica" or "Wareite". Both surfaces are easy to clean.

Is it possible to remove deep brown marks from the linoleum round the cooker?

Apply a hot solution of oxalic acid—1 part acid to 3 or 4 parts water and leave for a minute or two then rinse. Repeat if necessary. Keep the oxalic acid well away from children and animals as well as food because it is very poisonous.

What is the best way to remove brown marks from a brick fireplace?

Scrub thoroughly with hot water and a hard brush. If the marks still remain try a solution of hydrochloric acid—one part acid to six parts water, and apply to each brick, carefully avoiding the cement surrounding it which may disintegrate if the acid touches it. Rinse with several clean waters. Use thick rubber gloves when applying the acid and be extremely careful when using it because it is very poisonous and powerful in action.

How can I prevent my "wash leather" going stiff when I have washed it?

Rinse in warm water to remove the dirt then wash in warm soapy water. When quite clean wash in another clean soapy water, squeeze gently and pull into shape. Hang up to dry; when almost dry rumple between the hands to soften it. Always avoid rinsing in plain water.

How can I remove a tight glass stopper from a bottle?

It is usually sufficient to tie a piece of rag, wrung out in hot water, round the stopper and tap it very gently. A few drops of oil poured round the top will help to loosen the stopper more quickly.

Is there any way to revive a shopping basket which no longer responds to a scrub with soap and water?

Try a coat of good varnish or paint. I can recommend "Valspar" 2–4 hour lacquer for this job because I have used it for my own basket.

How should bamboo furniture be cleaned?

Wash it occasionally with soap and water, and polish with any good furniture cream.

What can I do to revive an old basketware chair which is looking shabby but is, oh! so comfortable?

Scrub the chair lightly with pure soap and water, paying particular attention to the small grooves where the dust and dirt accumulates. Rinse well. If the chair still does not satisfy you, give it a coat of paint or enamel, or plain colourless varnish.

We have bought a suite of upholstered "loom" furniture and I am wondering how this should be cleaned.

Dust the basketwork regularly with a very soft brush and when necessary, rub with a cloth wrung out in warm soapy water to freshen.

The seat of a cane chair has sagged through use. What can I do?

It is often possible to improve the shape by dabbing lightly with a cloth wrung out in hot soda water; treat both sides of the seat, pressing the underpart gently upwards as you work. Rub over with a dry cloth and dry thoroughly in the open air.

Is there any way to protect the lacquered back of a hairbrush while the brush is being washed?

Smear the back of the brush with vaseline before washing. It is unwise to wash hairbrushes very frequently because this is inclined to soften the bristles. The brushes can be cleaned between washings by careful combing with a fine tooth comb then rubbing with a soft, damp cloth.

I find that my long- and short-handled sweeping brushes are apt to go soft with continual washing. Is there any way of stiffening them after washing?

Add a little salt to the final rinsing water; 1 tablespoonful of salt to 2 pints of water is sufficient. Wash the brushes in warm soapy water to which a small lump of soda has been added; beat them up and down in the water till clean then rinse in several changes of clean warm water, and finally, in warm water containing salt. Shake off surplus water and hang up to dry so that the water does not soak into the wooden heads of the brushes.

What is the secret of keeping cut flowers fresh?

There are a number of ways by which you can preserve their freshness. Bruise hard stems and split soft stems so that they can absorb the water easily. Remove unwanted leaves below the water line as well as above it to relieve the stem of unnecessary burden and keep the water fresh. And when flowers have just been cut plunge them right up to their necks in fresh water for an hour or two before arranging them.

Is there any method of reviving flowers once they have begun to droop?

Yes, providing you tackle them before they have drooped too long. Lift them out of their vases and plunge the stems into fairly hot water—it should be of a temperature that your hand can bear comfortably—and remove after a few moments.

How can unpainted teak and oak garden furniture be preserved?

By rubbing over with a little linseed oil every few months. If it becomes dirty it can be rubbed with a little steel wool the way of the grain before the oil is applied.

Can you advise on treatment for the coachwork of

a new car? The lacquer has chipped badly in several places.

The chips can be treated by brushing on a lacquer made specially for cars, such as "Car-Lac", of the exact colour. If the chips are sufficiently bad to warrant an all-over coat of lacquer, apply with a spray instead of a brush, after fixing several thicknesses of newspaper or brown paper to the windows, windscreen, bonnet, etc., to prevent their getting sprayed with the paint.

I want to repaint the bath. How should I begin?

Remove all dirt and grease by washing down with a good paste cleanser like "Gumption" and dry thoroughly. Any rusty parts should be properly cleaned and touched up with the paint; "Trojax" is one good paint for this purpose. Paint the bath thinly allowing each coat to dry quite hard before applying the next coat. Apply as many coats as necessary to obtain the desired finish and see that the final coat is completely hard before using the bath.

Your advice, please, on the paint I should use on the inside of a fish pond that I am making. I am told the ordinary paints will kill the fish.

There is a special bituminous sealer on the market that does not affect the fish or the plant life of a pond. It is made by Spratts Patent Ltd.

My husband and I are trying to work out a practical budget. What percentage of the annual income should be allowed for the purchase and maintenance of the house, and for food, fuel, etc.?

This is a very difficult question to answer because so much depends upon circumstances. But as a general rule it is unwise to spend more than one-quarter of the total family income on the house rent, rates, mortgage payments and maintenance. Food should always be regarded as a major necessity and it is unwise to economise drastically on this commodity. Bearing this in mind between forty and forty-five per cent. of the family income can be allotted for food, laundry, lighting, fuel, "daily help," etc., etc.

I want to fit spark arresters to chimneys to help prevent the risk of fire damage to a thatched roof. What do you suggest?

There are several revolving type cowls on the market for this job that are passed by insurance companies. Alternatively, you could get a local builder to make and fix guards of galvanised wire, 1/16th inch mesh, which would be cheaper and quite efficient.

We had a bad fall of soot and some of it has worked its way into the pile of our light fawn carpet. How can I treat it?

Get rid of all the soot you can by putting the vacuum cleaner over the carpet, or brushing it thoroughly with a stiff brush, then rub with a soft cloth moistened with carbon tetrachloride. Repeat if necessary. If the remainder of the carpet looks faded in comparison to the cleaned part you can freshen it up with a little ammonia in warm water applied on a soft cloth. Allow 1 tablespoonful to 2 pints water and rub vigorously.

I was at a friend's house when her chimney caught fire and neither of us knew what to do. What is the routine?

Close all windows and doors. Put salt on the fire and remove as much of the fuel as possible. Roll back the carpet or rug and protect the hearth from burning soot. Do *not* pour water on the fire. If the fire continues call the fire brigade.

Our cold water system has frozen and I am frightened we may get a burst pipe when the thaw comes. What do you advise me to do?

Get a plumber NOW! Don't wait for the thaw! Burst pipes can cause considerable damage and should be avoided if at all possible. Let out the boiler because your hot water storage tank supply may be interrupted by the freeze-up. When the plumber has thawed out the pipes keep them open by running cold water through all the cold water taps and the lavatory cisterns at least once every three hours during the very frosty weather, and have as much heating as you are able in the house. If you install a heater in the loft this will help considerably but be careful to see it is completely safe and cannot accidentally cause a fire. When the plumber comes take note of the position of the freeze-up for future reference; lag it if possible and if in spite of precautions the pipe should freeze again you may be able to thaw it out with a lighted taper. Do NOT leave the taps dripping because the outlet may freeze and cause the water to overflow the sink and hand-basin and flood the kitchen and bathroom.

HOUSEHOLD CLEANING

Is there any way of preserving the appearance of a chromium plated letter-box?

Good quality chromium plate is one of the hardest wearing finishes there is and a rub with a soft duster is usually enough to keep it in good condition. A little furniture cream can be applied occasionally and the chromium well rubbed. Soap and water can be used to clean soiled chromium plated articles.

Our brass door knocker becomes tarnished very quickly in damp weather. Is there any way of preventing this happening?

Brass and copper ornaments and fittings can be painted with cellulose lacquer and can then be kept clean by rubbing with a soft cloth, and occasionally, a little furniture cream. Metal polish must never be used on a lacquered surface because it injures and eventually removes the lacquer.

Before applying the lacquer clean your door knocker with metal polish in the usual way till a high sheen is obtained. Then rub over with a soft cloth dipped in methylated spirits to remove all traces of grease. Apply the lacquer carefully, and avoid breathing on the work; it is important to choose a dry day to do it because any dampness will spoil the effect of the lacquer. When the first coat is thoroughly dry apply a second coat, making sure that the metal is completely covered all over.

Are the silver cleaning liquids like "Silver Dip" as good as the paste and liquid polishes for silver?

Liquids of this type are labour saving and effective for removing tarnish from silver but they must not be regarded as silver polishes. Small articles such as cutlery can be dipped in the wide necked bottles and larger articles are swabbed over with the liquid applied on a piece of cotton wool or other absorbent material. It is necessary to rinse the articles thoroughly if they happen to be cutlery, and to avoid spilling the liquid especially on stainless steel.

Can you tell me about the rust removers now on the market?

Most of these solutions are painted on the rusty articles and when dry the solution forms a protective coating that can then be painted over in the usual way or left uncovered. The manufacturers' directions should be carefully followed; in nearly all cases the liquid is best when applied hot (it can be heated in a jar in a pan of hot water). Because the liquid is poisonous it should never be used for baking utensils of any type—rusty baking tins must be discarded immediately the rust is detected.

How should baking tins be cleaned?

Wash the tins in the usual way, avoiding hard rubbing and harsh abrasives which scratch and wear down the coating. Dry very carefully to prevent rusting and, when possible, place upside down in a warm oven or on a plate warming rack to dry off.

If the tins are particularly dirty and greasy through lack of attention boil up a strong solution of soda in them, rinse thoroughly and dry well before putting away.

Can you wash up saucepans and baking tins in the dishwashing machines?

At the time of going to press, no! The dishwashing machines now on the market are intended for the fairly large household where they will cope adequately with the china, glass and cutlery, washing and rinsing them and, provided the water is hot enough, they usually dry in a moment or two and are ready to put away. I believe manufacturers are hoping to introduce a smaller model suitable for the small household in the future.

Is there any truth in the saying that aluminium saucepans are injurious to health?

According to a Ministry of Health investigation this is untrue except in isolated cases where people are allergic to this metal. It is true to say that an infinitesimal amount of the metal is absorbed during cooking, but according to the medical profession this is insufficient to cause concern about the use of aluminium cooking utensils.

What is the best way to clean aluminium saucepans?

Avoid using coarse abrasive cleansers on the inside of the pans because these are inclined to scratch and wear the surface, and the normally slight chemical reaction with the food is thereby increased. Use a stiff long-handled brush for the insides and fine wire wool for the outsides of the pans. When a pan becomes discoloured on the inside the original colour can be restored by boiling in it some acid fruit or a weak acid solution. Avoid using washing soda or abrasives at all times.

How can I get rid of the musty smell inside a vacuum flask that has not been used for some months? Also bits of brown skin float on the water when I fill it.

The musty smell is possibly due to the corks having been left in the flasks over the winter; they should always be removed. The brown skin is most likely the deposit left by strong tea that has begun to peel off the inside of the flask. Pour in a solution of bicarbonate of soda—2 teaspoonfuls to 1 pint of hot water, cork and leave to stand for 12 hours, then rinse thoroughly. The flask should then be quite sweet and clean.

What is the best way to clean a stainless steel sink?

Use hot water in which a little pure soap or soapless detergent has been dissolved and rub with a wad of soft cloth or a long-handled soft bristled pot brush. Stubborn marks can be removed with a non-scratchy paste cleanser like "Chemico" or "Gumption." Rinse with clean hot water.

We are moving into a new house and want to preserve the lovely glazed surface of the porcelain sink and hand-basin. How should these be cleaned? Can you give me any hints on cleaning the bath?

Clean with hot water using a little pure soap or soapless detergent and a wad of soft cloth or long-handled soft bristled brush. Occasionally you may need to use a chlorine bleach for the sink; follow the instructions on the label carefully and rinse extra well. The paste cleansers will keep your bath in good condition and the nylon mitts being sold in the shops are good for removing the water marks.

Is it possible to make an impregnated silver cleaning cloth at home?

Yes, but it is hardly worth the trouble because excellent impregnated cloths for silver cleaning can be bought in the shops quite cheaply. To make a cloth at home soak a square of good quality towelling in a solution of 2 tablespoonfuls of ammonia, 2 level teaspoonfuls of plate-powder and $\frac{3}{4}$ pint of water. Leave to soak for about an hour then dry off, and use to dry the silver after washing it. It will need resoaking in the ammonia-plate powder liquid each week or so if used regularly for cutlery.

How should stainless steel be cleaned?

Stainless steel does not require cleaning; a vigorous rub on a dry tea towel or soft cloth is sufficient to restore its appearance after washing.

Is there any way of reviving gilt picture frames?

Rub over with a cloth dipped in warm turpentine or turps. substitute. Warm in a basin of hot water, NEVER on a cooker because turpentine is highly inflammable.

A cure please, for discoloured piano keys.

Rub with a soft cloth moistened with methylated spirits. If the discoloration is particularly bad, the keys should be treated with hydrogen peroxide—20 vols, in the proportion of 1 part peroxide to 5 or 6 parts water. This should be rinsed off well and dried. In both cases great care should be taken to avoid any of the liquid running down between the keys.

Can playing cards be cleaned?

Rub with breadcrumbs or precipitated whiting. Avoid india rubber which roughens them and makes them difficult to handle.

How can I clean a rush mat?

Put the vacuum cleaner over it to remove dust and grit then scrub with soap and water. Dry thoroughly before putting down again on the floor.

There are some blue-green marks on the bath caused, I think, by our copper geyser. How should they be treated?

Sprinkle a little vinegar on a soft cloth and rub the marks then rinse away quickly. Repeat as often as necessary, keeping off the unmarked surrounds as far as possible.

How can a fawn-coloured canvas grip bag be cleaned?

Rub over with a damp cloth and leave to dry. If the grip is very dirty wash it with a cloth wrung out in plenty of lather—either soap or soapless detergent—and rinse with a cloth wrung out in clean warm water. If the grip is lined avoid wetting the canvas sufficiently for it to penetrate to the lining and spoil this. Dry if possible in the open air.

How can discoloured flower vases be cleaned?

Place a little vinegar and silver sand in them, shake well and leave on one side for an hour or two, shaking often. Rub round with a cloth before rinsing and drying.

Is it possible to brighten old bronze ornaments?

It would be wrong for them to look too bright but you can cheer them up by sprinkling a little almond or olive oil on to a soft cloth and rubbing this all over your bronze ornaments. Remove all the oil with a soft duster; this treatment may be repeated at regular intervals, and in the meantime a rub with a soft duster will keep the ornaments fresh. Use a brush to clean the ornamental parts.

I have been given an alabaster statuette. How should it be cleaned?

Alabaster can be washed in warm soapy water, then thoroughly dried and polished. Any stains can usually be removed with a pad of flannel moistened with turpentine and dipped in powdered pumice stone; the alabaster must then be washed with water to which a little borax has been added, dried and polished.

How is one supposed to clean pewter?

Get some finely powdered whiting and mix with a little oil to a paste. Apply with a piece of soft cloth and rub well then polish with a clean cloth.

Is there any method of removing stubborn fly marks from electric lamps? I have some that refuse to move through ordinary washing.

Rub the lamps carefully with a soft cloth moistened with a few drops of methylated spirits.

What is the best way to keep electric lamps clean? Can they be washed?

Yes, wash them in soapy water but do not wet the caps.

How can I prevent dirty marks appearing on the walls above the small wall brackets?

Fill in beneath the shades with discs of white diffusing plastic.

How can lampshades be cleaned?

Turn off the light at the switch and remove the shade.

Glass: Wash in warm soapy water and polish with a soft, dry cloth.

Parchment: Wipe with a clean cloth, wrung out in a weak solution of vinegar and water, then with a little soda and water. Wring out the cloth quite tightly before touching the parchment in each case. Leave to dry thoroughly before handling again.

Paper: Do not apply moisture to paper or it may buckle. Brush with a soft bristled brush and dust; dirty marks can often be removed with an artist's cleaning rubber.

Buckram: Clean with the extension brush attachment on the vacuum cleaner. Or use a soft bristled brush.

Plastic: Rub with a cloth wrung out in soapy water and then with a clean damp cloth. Do not rub dry.

Silk: It is safer to have silk shades dry cleaned.

Fabric: If the fabric is washable these shades can be dipped in warm soapy water then rinsed in clean water and dried quickly, preferably in the open air, before the frame can rust and mark the material.

Can you advise on the removal of heat marks from a dining table?

If the table is french polished rub the marks quite vigorously with a soft pad moistened with three drops of methylated spirits, working with a circular movement. Metal polish is better than methylated spirits for a table with a shiny cellulose finish.

I accidentally spilled a few drops of perfume on my highly-polished dressing table. Can I remove the marks?

Treat as for heat marks above.

I would like to know how to remove greasy marks from upholstered furniture.

Dab with a grease solvent like carbon tetrachloride, working from well outside the greasy mark in a circular movement towards the mark; this way you should be able to obviate a ring appearing round the part that has been cleaned.

One hears a lot about silicones being used in furniture and floor polishes. What are the advantages of them?

Silicones are water and dirt repellants and when used in polishes they leave a hard, lasting finish. Silicone wax polishes are available for floors and creams for furniture and paintwork. A coating is spread on the wood and left to dry for a few moments before rubbing with a clean, soft cloth. The polish it leaves will last for several months without further application.

How can marks be removed from wallpaper?

Non-greasy marks usually respond to a gentle rub with a soft india rubber, and all-over grubbiness can be removed with "Decomin" wallpaper cleanser.

I want to put a patch on our dining-room wall which is papered and has unfortunately collected a greasy mark in a very prominent position. Please tell me how to do this.

Remove the stained paper after wetting it with warm water. Cut a new piece of wallpaper a little larger than the pieces you have removed and tear the edges roughly so that they are ragged looking. Paste in position. Providing the surrounding wallpaper has not faded the patch should be almost invisible.

I would like a copy of your stain removal chart.

Acid Stain: Treat with a weak solution of washing soda, using 1 teaspoonful soda *or* 1 teaspoonful borax, to 1 pint water.

Blacklead: Rub carefully with turpentine, and if at all possible, wash the article that is stained.

Blood: Sponge it as soon as possible with salt and warm water—1 oz. salt to 1 pint water, and rinse well. In the case of a bloodstain that has dried, soak it in this solution for 2 hours or more then wash well, using soap and water, and rinse very well.

Blue: If you get a stain due to the use of too much laundry blue, soak in vinegar and water till the colour comes out. Or if very bad bleach with a product like" Domestos" or "Parazone". This treatment applies only to linen and cottons.

Coffee: If the stain is "set in" the material soak in glycerine then sponge with borax and warm water. Wash in the usual way.

Creosote: Rub with benzene.

Egg: Egg yolk can usually be removed by sponging with soap and water, and any remaining mark can be treated with grease solvent. Egg white can usually be removed by sponging with warm salt and water—1 oz. to 1 pint of water.

Fruit: Soak the material for 5 to 10 minutes in borax and water, using about ½ teaspoonful of borax to ½ pint of water. Rinse well. It may be necessary to rub the article slightly when in the borax water to get rid of the stain completely. Treat as soon as possible after the stain appears.

Ice-Cream: Sponge immediately with warm water and rinse in clean water. If any mark remains let it dry and rub lightly with a grease solvent, like carbon tetrachloride.

Indelible Pencil: This can nearly always be removed with methylated spirits, but if the material is rayon, test an unimportant part to make sure it will "take" this treatment—not all rayons will do so.

Ink: Ordinary writing ink stains can usually be removed with oxalic acid or salts of lemon, but both these chemicals are very poisonous and must be used very carefully and the material rinsed thoroughly (see *Ironmould*). Test an unimportant part before applying the chemicals to the stained area. *Red ink* often responds to treatment with borax and water. *Marking ink* can sometimes be removed with hydrogen peroxide with a solution of permanganate of potash used alternately in the proportion of $\frac{1}{2}$ teaspoonful permanganate to 1 pint water and 1 teaspoonful peroxide to 4 teaspoonfuls of water. *Ball-point pen ink* usually dissolves under methylated spirit. *Ink stains on furniture* can generally be removed with a weak oxalic acid solution—$\frac{1}{4}$ teaspoonful oxalic acid to $\frac{1}{4}$ pint warm water, applied with a tiny brush, and washed off carefully. Test rayons first.

Iodine: Use a fairly week solution of photographer's "hypo" to remove iodine stains—about $\frac{1}{2}$ teaspoonful dissolved in $\frac{1}{2}$ pint of water. Soak the stained article in this for a minute or so, then rinse in the usual way. Diluted ammonia can also be used for this purpose. Test rayons first.

Ironmould: Apply a hot solution of oxalic acid or salts of lemon— $\frac{1}{2}$ teaspoonful to $\frac{1}{2}$ pint hot water. Leave for a few minutes then rinse extra well. Test coloureds and rayons first.

Grass: Sponge or soak for a short time in methylated spirits. Test rayons first.

Grease: Grease and oil stains can usually be removed with carbon tetrachloride or cleaning benzine.

Lipstick: Soap and water usually remove these efficiently. But if they are stubborn sponge with carbon tetrachloride.

Mud: Leave to dry thoroughly then brush off.

Nail Polish: Treat with acetone or other nail polish remover, finishing with methylated spirits, but be careful about rayon materials some of which do not stand up to this treatment.

Nicotine: Sponge with methylated spirits, but be careful about rayons and test before you use it on the main part of this material.

Paint: Enamel paint can be removed by treating with turpentine which should be applied as soon as possible. Oil paint will also respond to turps. Cellulose paint stains can be removed with acetone. Again, be careful about rayons (see above).

C

Rouge: Paste and powder rouge stains can be treated with a grease solvent, and any remaining marks removed with methylated spirits. Test rayons first.

Rust: A solution of oxalic acid or salts of lemon—$\frac{1}{2}$ teaspoonful to $\frac{1}{2}$ pint hot water, usually removes rust marks on fabric. But if the material is coloured test before treating to see the colours and material will stand up to the acid. Rinse extra well.

Scorch marks can be treated when only slight, by sponging with borax and water then rinsing well—$\frac{1}{2}$ teaspoonful borax to $\frac{1}{2}$ pint water. But rub very gently because the material will be thinned by the scorching. Heavy materials that have become scorched should be brushed before treating to remove loose bits of wool, etc.

Sealing wax: Rub with methylated spirits. Test rayon first.

Sea water: Sponge several times with warm water to get rid of the salt and the material should dry satisfactorily. Leather shoes can be treated with hot milk and soda—1 teaspoonful soda to 5 or 6 teaspoonfuls of milk. When dry, polish in the usual way.

Shoe polish: Treat with turpentine, finishing off with a little methylated spirits if any colour remains. Test rayons first.

Soot: Remove all soot you can by brushing or vacuuming or shaking, then treat with carbon tetrachloride.

Tar: Remove as much of the tar as you can with a knife then rub with a cloth dipped in carbon tetrachloride.

Tea: When fresh, a good washing in hot soapy water will usually remove the stain; boiling will help remove more stubborn stains. Stains which have been there some time should be treated with borax—$\frac{1}{2}$ teaspoonful to $\frac{1}{2}$ pint water. Rinse well after treatment. Very delicate lacy fabrics, etc., should be sent to the cleaners for expert treatment.

Tobacco: Treat with methylated spirits. Test rayons first.

Tomato: Remove with borax and water—$\frac{1}{2}$ teaspoonful to $\frac{1}{2}$ pint water. Rinse extra well after treating.

Wine: Use a hot solution of borax and water—$\frac{1}{2}$ teaspoonful of borax to $\frac{1}{2}$ pint hot water and soak the material in this till cool.

Old wine stains on cotton and linen materials can be bleached with diluted chlorine which should be well rinsed away afterwards, this must *not* be used for rayon, woollen or silk materials.

WASHING AND IRONING

I find it is often impossible to recognise the basic material from which many of the new fabrics are made and I am "at sea" when it comes to laundering them. How does one know when a garment should be washed and when it should be dry cleaned?

I agree it is very difficult to recognise the familiar materials when they appear with a new finish and, unfortunately, all manufacturers have not yet complied with the housewives' earnest request that laundering instructions should be issued with all materials and garments.

It is always safer to buy branded goods with an established reputation; the manufacturers often declare the name of the material on the label. When in doubt, wash a small portion of the material that doesn't matter so much—a belt for instance; if you are still unsure, or cannot test, play safe and take it to the cleaners, explaining your doubts to the assistant who will make a special note on the ticket that goes with the garment to the factory, asking for special care to be taken.

I never seem able to get my laundry really white. Why is it?

Hard water is one cause of grey clothes. The hard water reacts with the soap to produce lime scum which settles on the clothes and is very difficult to rinse away. The washing water can be softened with "Calgon" to overcome this trouble. *Dirty washing water* is another cause of greyness. If the clothes are very dirty they should be put through a second soapy water. It is a bad thing to wash too many clothes in the same water whether by hand or machine; in a machine the clothes must have room to move freely.

Insufficient rinsing is another cause of greyness. Two, three or more rinsing waters should be used if necessary to remove all traces of soap. Wring before rinsing to get rid of the soapy water.

Lack of boiling can also cause greyness. Although clothes can be kept a reasonably good colour for quite a long time without boiling my experience shows that an occasional boil is essential. Two teaspoonfuls of borax added to the soapy water in the boiler has a whitening effect and is harmless. Alternatively, one of the chemical bleaches may be used occasionally but they tend to weaken the fabrics if used regularly. Blue helps to counteract yellowness but does not help at all in combating greyness. For slight bleaching, oxygen soap powders have a valuable whitening effect. Do not boil or bleach rayon, wool or nylon fabrics.

Drying the clothes indoors is another cause of greyness. The sunshine is a wonderful bleacher and clothes should be hung out of doors to dry whenever possible. Discoloured "whites" can be given a harmless sun bleach this way; spread the wet articles on a clean sheet on the lawn and as soon as they dry damp them down; repeat the damping down once or twice more before bringing the articles indoors.

I have read about "optical bleaches" that are used in the modern soap powders and I am wondering if they are harmful to the clothes?

There is no evidence that these traces of fluorescent chemicals in washing powders are harmful to fabrics. They are really a colourless blueing agent which give the appearance of whiteness by emitting bluish fluorescence. They mask rather than cure any discoloration of the fabrics.

How much borax is necessary to soften the water; is it a good water softener?

You need approximately $\frac{1}{2}$ oz. borax to each gallon of water but the amount varies according to the hardness of the water. It is recommended for use with delicate fabrics in preference to washing soda which is a more effective, but also more drastic, water softener.

Is it wise to use a water softener in hard water districts?

Yes, it makes wash day much easier and the soap goes further in softened water. "Calgon" is a good powdered water softener and you need about 1 tablespoon to soften 9-11 gallons of water according to how hard the water is in your district.

Do you recommend soapless detergents in a hard water area?

They are useful for certain purposes in hard water areas because they do not react with hard water salts to make lime curd. Follow the manufacturers' instructions and do not use more than is necessary.

My skin is very dry and my hands react badly to wash day especially when I use soapless detergents. Can you advise me?

You need a barrier cream to prevent the detergents removing the natural oils from your skin. Innoxa do excellent barrier creams, one for dry work and another for wet work. Apply it before you begin the job and it will protect your hands for several hours. Alternatively, you can wear rubber gloves or plastic mitts to protect your hands.

The oxygen bleach type of soap powders seem to be very powerful. Do you recommend them?

They serve a useful purpose when washing heavily soiled articles and for overnight soaking to loosen the dirt.

Do you recommend the chemical bleaching preparations for home laundering?

Provided these are used only occasionally they are useful but when used regularly they are likely to weaken the fabrics. Regular boiling keeps clothes white and will not weaken the fabrics.

Which is the best—soap or detergent?

Both have their points. Detergents are useful in hard water areas because with them, there is no formation of lime scum which is inclined to settle on the clothes and is hard to get rid of, especially in the case of woollens. Another advantage is that detergents dissolve in cool or lukewarm water which is valuable for washing coloured articles which are inclined to lose colour or bleed in hot water.

Soap is recommended for heavily soiled articles which need hand rubbing because its lubricating qualities reduce wear and tear of the fabric. Soap is an excellent cleanser and its good suspending properties help to prevent the dirt settling again on the clothes when it has been removed. Soap is also valuable when a solid (as against a powdered cleanser) is required, for example, when scrubbing.

With detergents, it is most important not to use more than is necessary and recommended by the manufacturers.

For how long should clothes be boiled?

This depends upon how dirty they are. Handkerchiefs and other small articles which are not badly discoloured should be boiled for between 10 and 15 minutes. Articles that are boiled only occasionally need longer—slow "stewing" for $\frac{1}{2}$ to 1 hour. A little borax added to the water will help to get them a good colour.

Is there any method of insuring against colours running when coloured material is being washed?

A little salt added to the washing water helps to prevent colours running but this should be used only with soapless detergents—not with soap because it kills soapy lather.

Should clothes be wrung before rinsing as well as after. If so, why?

Clothes should be wrung before rinsing because otherwise if the water is hard, greyish marks, due to soap curd, may spoil the appearance of the clothes, and no amount of rinsing will remove them. This way you will have cleaner rinsing water, too.

Does washing harm corsets?

No, and washing is the best way of cleaning them. Never allow them to become very soiled and wash often in warm, soapy water, using a soft nail brush to remove obstinate marks. Rinse in several clean waters, pat out the moisture with an absorbent towel then hang out to dry in the open air. Press lightly while damp, using a cool iron and avoiding the elastic parts.

Is there any way of reviving the dye that is faded through perspiration stain?

You can sponge the stained part with ammonia, or vinegar, and water but first, test the material by applying some of this solution to a part of the garment that does not matter, such as the hem turning. The odour of perspiration can be removed from washable materials by soaking in a solution of borax and water— 1 tablespoonful borax to 1 pint water. Rinse well.

How does one test material for colour fastness?

Take a small piece of the material, preferably a belt or cuff, and test by wetting in cold or tepid water, laying a small piece of white material over it and the pressing with a warm iron. If it leaves only a very faint mark or no colour at all, the garment may safely be washed.

The colours of my new printed floral dress "run" badly when washed and I am scared to wash another similar dress in case the same thing happens.

This trouble of colour bleeding is much less common now than it was a year or two ago, but there is still need to exercise the greatest care when washing all new brightly-coloured prints. Use tepid water and a detergent with a little salt (the salt must never be used with soap, only with detergents). Rinse at once in clean tepid water, wring and remove as much of the water as possible in a rough towel then hang up to dry in the open air at once.

How should rayon materials be washed and ironed?

Do not use bleach or starch. Do not boil or rub hard. Thoroughly dissolve a small amount of soap flakes or washing powder in warm (not hot) water, and tumble the material about in the water till it is clean. Rinse well in at least two warm waters, and wring by hand or with the aid of a rubber-rollered wringer (avoiding putting a garment bearing buttons or fasteners through the wringer for fear of their cutting into the material).

If the garment is too dry for ironing re-wet all over and do not just sprinkle with water; get the iron warm, and keep at a low temperature to begin with, with the thermostat set to "rayon". Increase the heat if necessary, also if you are a very quick ironer. Be careful not to press fasteners, buttons or seams into the fabric.

Iron on the wrong side; press out excess moisture from taffetas and satins in a towel and iron almost wet. Press heavy spun rayons under a damp cloth. Crêpes have a tendency to shrink when wet and garments made from crêpe should be allowed to dry before gently pulling into shape under the iron. Exceptions are the rayon crêpes guaranteed against shrinkage; these do not require this special treatment.

Your tips on washing pure silk, please!

Do not wash in very hot water and never soak or boil it, or wash in a washing machine. Squeeze gently in warm soap suds without rubbing or twisting. Rinse twice in warm water, roll in a towel and pat out the excess moisture then dry in an airy place away from sun or direct heat. When almost dry iron on the wrong side with a warm iron; shantung, tussore and douppion should be ironed when quite dry to prevent shine.

My children's woollies shrink badly after a few washings, and they are often too tight for them to wear. What causes shrinkage and how can it be avoided?

Woollens shrink when an unsuitable detergent containing a lot of soda or other alkali is used; when insufficient soap or soapless detergent is used and the clothes are rubbed instead of tossed about in the washing water; when they are insufficiently rinsed; when they are dried quickly before an open fire; when they are ironed with a hot iron.

Wash in pure soap or suitable detergent, and see that the rinsing water is of similar temperature to the washing waters. Rinse in several waters. Dry in the open air and press, when almost dry, with a cool iron.

What makes woollens go yellow and what is the cure?

Excessive heat, either indoors or very hot sunshine out of doors, will cause this trouble, and so will unsuitable washing powders, and unsoftened hard water. It helps to add a little borax to the washing water and/or a trace of blue to the rinsing water. If very badly discoloured soak in a solution of hydrogen peroxide and ammonia—$\frac{1}{2}$ pint of 10-vol. peroxide to $\frac{1}{2}$ gallon water, and 1 teaspoonful ammonia—for $\frac{1}{2}$ hour then rinse well before drying.

Is there any way of treating felted, shrunken woollies?

Try washing in a soapless detergent then rinsing extra well, and taking care to pull the garment into shape while wet, pinning it in shape and drying this way, in the open air.

New woollens seem to "eat up" the soapy lather. Why is this?

They often contain a certain amount of acid which destroys the lather; add a little ammonia to the washing water to correct this when washing new woollies; rinse extra well.

Do you recommend the washing of hand-knitted garments and loosely woven materials in a washing machine?

Generally, no! I think these garments keep their shape better when washed in pure soap flakes by hand, and rinsed in several clean waters of similar temperature.

What is the best way to prevent men's woollen socks from shrinking in the wash?

Use fairly hot water and the necessary amount of soap flakes, soap powder or soapless detergent, and rinse in several waters of similar temperature (the similar temperature is important). Squeeze most of the water out and dry on wire frame sock dryers of the proper size. Hang on a line out of doors or indoors away from direct heat.

Can you advise on the washing of rugs?

Sheepskin and wool rugs can be washed successfully at home. Wash in plenty of lukewarm soapy water; squeeze and knead rather than rub them to remove the dirt, press out the soap suds carefully before rinsing in several waters of similar temperature then press out as much moisture as possible, shake thoroughly and dry slowly on a breezy day spread across two lines. Shake often during drying and knead to prevent the rug going hard while it is drying. Add 2 oz. emulsified olive oil to washing water for sheepskins.

Can I wash an eiderdown successfully at home?

Providing the eiderdown is of the washable type you should be able to wash it quite successfully at home. Choose a sunny, breezy day. Press the eiderdown up and down gently in lukewarm soapy water for a few minutes and then press out most of the suds and rinse in three clear, lukewarm waters. Do *not* wring. Dry

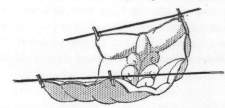

over two lines and shake often while drying to loosen the feathers. Turn several times. Iron lightly when dry, using a warm iron. By sewing tapes to each corner the eiderdown can be pegged by the tapes to a double line so that the wind can blow all round.

Have you any special tips on washing loose covers at home?

Make sure the material is washable before attempting to launder it. Cretonnes, rayons, slubbs, brocades all wash well in lukewarm soapy water. Begin by shaking the covers to remove the dirt then immerse them in the soapy water and scrub the very dirty parts gently with a soft brush. You may need to put the covers through a second soapy water if they are rather grubby. Rinse and wring twice to get rid of all the soapy water. Iron when nearly dry and finish the ironing when the covers are back on the furniture. Cottons and linens look nicer and keep clean longer when they are lightly starched.

I want to wash my blankets in a way that will make them look really fluffy and fresh. Please advise me how to wash them.

It is important to use plenty of soap flakes, soap powder or soapless detergent; otherwise the blankets will dry flat and rather hard. New blankets will seem to "eat up" the lather at once and you need a second soapy water to wash them in. Avoid rubbing; this is most important. Press the blanket gently up and down in the washing water and squeeze gently till all the dirt is out. Put the blanket through a loose rubber wringer and then rinse at least three times in plenty of lukewarm water—see that the temperature is similar to that in which they were washed. Wring between each rinse for ease of handling. Dry over two clothes lines if possible, so that the wind can get all round and underneath the blanket. Try not to peg unless it is a very windy day, and shake several times during drying to keep it fluffy. Press silk bindings with a warm iron when dry.

My three-year-old blankets have lost a lot of their fluffiness. Can I restore them? Rub over lightly with a fine wire brush, a small section at a time.

What is the best way to wash nylon stockings?

Use pure soap or soapless detergent and hot water, and DO wash soon after each wearing. Squeeze gently in the soap suds without rubbing or wringing. Rinse in clean water of similar temperature and dry away from artificial heat and direct sunlight. When hung to dry over a wooden rail it is advisable to place a piece of cotton or plastic over the rail to prevent the threads being pulled accidentally by rough wood.

Can glazed chintz be laundered at home?

Only if you have the special glossing iron with convex base which is necessary to restore the finish. Glazed chintz is now nearly always sent to a reliable dry cleaners.

Can moiré fabric be washed at home?

Real silk moiré is best sent to the dry cleaners, but artificial silk moiré can be washed; follow instructions for washing rayon.

Your advice please on washing fine lace table mats.

Wash in lukewarm soapy water, rinse well and dry flat. Iron over a soft pad.

Do you recommend that embroidered curtains, covers and chair backs should be washed at home?

Providing the material is a washable type these can be washed at home successfully in warm soapy water. Iron on the wrong side over a thick pad of material to prevent flattening the embroidery.

Is it advisable to wash plush and velvet at home?

Most of these pile fabrics wash well in lukewarm soapy water. They should be washed quickly, continuously moved about in the soapy water, and well rinsed. Excess moisture should be removed at once by rolling in a towel or putting through a wringer. Hang to dry rather slowly away from direct sunlight or a fire.

How should net, lace, marquisette and ninon curtains be washed?

These need very careful handling. Fold long curtains in four and tie loosely with tapes to prevent them pulling out of shape or tearing under the weight of the water. If very dirty, rinse in plain water then soak in lukewarm soapy water for $\frac{1}{2}$ hour before washing carefully in lukewarm soapy water, kneading and squeezing but not twisting. Rinse well. Remove the ties and dry; iron with a warm iron while slightly damp. Stretch gently except near the edges. Nylon ninon requires only very light pressing. It is impossible to guard against slight shrinkage and this should be allowed for when the curtains are made.

How should bedspreads be washed?

When made of cotton, linen, rayon or candlewick, wash in lukewarm soapy water, squeeze gently but do not rub. Rinse in three clean waters of similar temperature and dry in the open air. Iron or press in the way recommended for the particular type of material.

I find that some garments, especially those "cut on the cross" such as underskirts, hang unevenly after laundering;

woollen jumpers and cardigans often become too wide in the body and the sleeves are too long. Can this be prevented?

It is often possible to avoid the hem of bias-cut garments from hanging unevenly by ironing along the weave, and never across—this is a golden rule which should be applied to all material most particularly bias-cut garments. Crêpe-finished materials, especially rayons, require a certain amount of pressure during ironing to restore the shape. Woollen garments, especially hand-knitteds, should be spread out on a flat surface to dry to avoid them stretching while wet; clothes drying hammocks of the same design as the old-fashioned string garden hammock are excellent for drying woollens both indoors and out of doors.

I find rayons "spot" when they are damped down. How can this be avoided?

It is advisable not to damp down rayon; if you cannot catch it when it is just right for ironing wet the material all over by plunging it into the washtub again, and iron before it gets quite dry.

I never seem able to damp down my laundry evenly and end up by getting one patch too wet and another too dry.

Try using a sprinkler. There is a good plastic one costing under 1s. which is attached to a cork suitable for fitting into a medicine bottle. This makes damping down very much more simple and satisfactory.

Can you give me any general tips about ironing?

Iron all double parts first, including pockets and hems, and inner side seams, also collars, sleeves and belts.

Generally, articles should be ironed selvedgewise, along their length—exceptions include many rayons which should be ironed across their width to restore their shape. Net curtains should be ironed diagonally across the weave to prevent ironing out of shape.

If there is a correct way to iron a blouse please describe it.

Iron the double parts first—the hem, seams, yoke, etc., ironing on the wrong side. Iron the sleeves next; unless a sleeveboard is available, fold the sleeves at the seams and iron to within $\frac{1}{2}$ inch of the outer fold on both sides of each sleeve. Open up the sleeve and finish the un-ironed part. Pay special attention to the top of the sleeve. Iron the collar next, first on the wrong side then finish it off on the right side.

Arrange the blouse on a board so that the bottom lies at your right hand. Begin ironing the right front and moving the work away from you, iron round the body of the blouse to the left front. Stretch and iron the front bands, longways. Any tucks or unpressed pleats need special attention. Re-iron any parts that have got creased and air off the blouse on a hanger.

How should a man's shirt be ironed?

Begin on the collar or collarband, ironing both inside and outside, and holding the material taut to prevent wrinkles, then iron the cuffs the same way. Then the sleeves, laid flat on the ironing board with the seam at one edge. Slip the body part over the ironing board so that you have it single thickness; begin on the yoke and button-hole strip then iron the fronts and back. Finish by fastening the buttons and giving the front a final quick press. Fold up the shirt by laying it face downwards on the board, fold back about a third from each side of the body, laying the sleeves flat then fold up the "tail" into three.

I accidentally pressed a woollen skirt, unprotected by a pressing cloth, on the right side and there is now a shiny patch. Can this be removed?

Providing you have not singed the material it should be possible to revive it by holding over the spout of a kettle of boiling water for several seconds, then brushing with a stiff brush against the nap. Repeat if necessary.

Is there any way to prevent shiny patches on rayon when ironing?

Always iron on the wrong side and use a cool iron. Iron the material in single thicknesses only.

Should permanently glazed chintz be ironed the right or wrong side?

Iron on the right side while it is still damp.

Do you advise storing linen in an airing cupboard?

No! The continual heat weakens the fibres and reduces the life of the linen considerably. It is better to store linen in a cupboard that is unheated and set apart for the job, and use the airing cupboard to air linen for immediate needs.

I have dyed a dress according to the dye manufacturer's instructions but it has come out unevenly, one part a strong colour, another hardly dyed at all. What went wrong?

This could be due to one of several factors. Was the container too small? Did you have insufficient liquid to cover the dress? Did you fail to stir all the time during dyeing? Did you fail to damp the dress evenly before dyeing? Did you wring the garment tightly when it came out of the bath? Did you keep wringing it to get it dry more quickly after you had hung it to dry? Avoid these faults next time and you will be successful.

Can you dye rayon?

This depends on the type; some rayons do not dye easily by home methods so choose a special dye and study the manufacturer's instructions. Test a small piece first before risking the whole garment; articles that cannot be dyed can usually be tinted a pastel shade.

What makes a dyed garment go streaky and spotty when it dries?

Most often it is due to the dye not being properly dissolved. Other times it is due to traces of grease being left on the fabric before dyeing—articles to be dyed should be well washed and rinsed to make sure that no dirt or grease remains.

FURNISHING

I have been disappointed when choosing colours for my basement sitting-room which has to be lit by electric light all the time. Can you give me a guide to the colour changes in electric light?

Always take your proposed purchases to a part of the shop where they can be seen under electric light before buying them. As a rough guide, you can reckon that dark greens look almost black, purples appear dark brown, reds take on an orangey hue, yellow is less bright and greens and blues look duller.

We find it difficult to decide where we are going to place the furniture in a new flat we shall be moving into.

The best way out of this difficulty is to make a plan of your new flat; reduce the size of the rooms and the furniture to go in them to scale of one-half or one-quarter inch to a square foot on squared paper. Then you will be able to "try" the furniture in various positions without unnecessary labour of moving it around when you get into the flat.

Do you agree that a fireplace should be treated as the focal point in a room even when it is not in use?

Yes! Place your chairs, tables and lamps around it, and arrange logs in the empty grate with a bowl of flowers on the corner of the hearth. A lovely picture or mirror hung over the fireplace enhances the appearance and strengthens the position of the fireplace as the focal point. Occasionally, when there are some big windows and a lovely view beyond, it is possible to make the windows the focal point instead of the disused fireplace; this should be done very carefully or you end up by having two focal points vying with each other!

Our living-room is very long and narrow. Can you advise on the grouping of furniture?

You can make the room appear shorter and therefore, wider, by placing the large pieces of furniture at the extreme ends of the room. Alternatively, furniture can be placed at intervals along the long walls to extend into the room and break up the length.

We have insufficient furniture for the very large sitting room in the house we are renting. Can you suggest ways of emphasising what we have got? We want to make the room appear cosier and smaller.

Paint the walls and woodwork warm, dark and contrasting colours. Reds and yellows are warm colours. Dark shades of these colours and low lights will help considerably to draw the walls of the room around you to give the impression of snugness. For example, deep red walls and off-white woodwork would decrease the size of the room considerably—visually!

I want to redecorate and refurnish a small sitting-room to make it appear larger than it actually is. What colours should I choose?

Choose cool colours—blue or blue-green and off-white. Cool colours appear to recede and walls painted in cool colours also recede to give the impression of extra space in the room. Avoid sharply contrasting colour schemes which tend to make a room appear smaller than it is. Another way (which is rather un-imaginative) is to paint the walls, ceiling and woodwork all in one colour; this gives the appearance of extra height as well as breadth to a room.

The use of a plain in preference to a patterned surface is another way to make a room appear larger; one or two medium-sized pictures can be hung but centre light fittings and side brackets should be avoided because they act as patterns and detract from the size of the room. Mirrors help to create an impression of spaciousness by reflection.

Plain rugs and carpets, plain upholstery and curtains,

plain bedspreads all help to increase the apparent size of a room.

I want to give an impression of additional space to our future living-room which is small. How should I furnish it?

Keep the centre of the room as clear as possible; lounge chairs or occasional chairs are preferable to wing chairs, and those without arms are best of all. Choose if you can a drawleaf or folding table and place it against a wall. Long, low bookshelves, window

seat and cupboards of similar height, and perhaps a divan all against the walls will lend size to the room. Avoid big-patterned or multi-coloured upholstery, curtains or carpet and keep the walls and paintwork as plain as possible. Avoid breaking the height of the room with a picture rail.

The exact opposite applies when a room is large and you want to break up the space to avoid coldness and the "ballroom appearance".

What are the main points to watch when buying furnishing fabric?

Try to find the answers to the following questions: Are the colours fast? Are they resistant to sunlight? Is the material pre-shrunk? Is the finish permanent, semi-permanent or temporary? (For example, wax and starch finishes need to be replaced at each laundering.) Is the material of the right weight for the purpose you have in mind? Is it closely woven and likely to withstand wear without losing shape?

Have you any suggestions for making a room appear longer than it actually is?

Choose furniture with long, low lines and arrange down the long walls. For example, long, low bookshelves and a long,

narrow window seat or divan can help considerably to give an appearance of extra length to a room.

What is the ideal position for a dressing table and writing desk in relation to the window?

The dressing table should be placed so that the light falls on the person and not on the mirror, and a writing desk should be placed sideways to the window so that the light falls on the desk from the writer's left side.

Should beds be placed against the walls or in the middle of the room?

This depends on the size of the bedroom. A small bedroom looks much larger if the bed is placed against a wall; in the case of twin beds, if they are arranged at right angles in a corner leaving the middle of the room free to give a feeling of spaciousness. Beds without footboards are especially suitable for a small room because the footboard fences off part of the room and makes it appear smaller than it actually is.

I am told that a veneered table top is better than a solid piece of wood. Is this true?

Yes, because the cross-graining of the layers ensures against warping which is always a point you need to watch when buying furniture.

When you go to buy a piece of furniture is there any quick way on checking that it is well made and worth buying?

Look at the back and undersides of drawers and the bottoms of chair seats; these should be well finished and never rough. Check that the drawers run smoothly and that the front of the drawer is dovetailed into the sides. The corner blocks of chairs, tables and cupboards, etc., should be glued and screwed in, not just nailed. And, of course, look at the general design and finish to make sure that these are practical and satisfactory in every way; for example, a table with splayed, thin legs cannot be as strong as a table of traditional design with straight solid legs. Points like this, may, or may not, matter; it all depends upon your individual requirements, and the kind of usage it is likely to receive.

I quite like a piece of veneered furniture but I suppose this is my bad taste and that I really ought to choose solid wood in preference to veneered furniture every time.

Not at all! It is a common fallacy that the use of veneer is a mark of inferior quality, but in fact all furniture that relies for its decoration on matched graining must be veneered because this is the only way matched graining can be produced. Cross-graining in, for example, a table, is preferable because it prevents warping.

I notice that in a suite of mahogany furniture we have just bought the drawers and shelves are made of oak. Does this indicate inferior quality?

On the contrary. The oak has been chosen to give greater strength and longer life and indicates shrewd judgment and high quality.

BEDDING

I am rather ignorant about mattresses. What kind do you recommend?

This is very much a personal matter. A slim person requires a mattress with more "give" in it than a heavier person. A good mattress is sufficiently buoyant to support every part of the body. You can choose between (1) an interior spring mattress with pocketed springs—this is silent and gives excellent spinal support; (2) an open coil interior spring mattress; (3) an upholstered mattress filled with wool and/or hair; (4) a rubber mattress. Try all these and decide which is most suited to your own particular needs. See it is both long enough and wide enough for your comfort.

I advise you to visit the London Bedding Centre, at Knightsbridge, London, S.W., and see the various types there. Alternatively, if you cannot get into London, your local retailer will I am sure, be pleased to advise you.

Is it advisable to turn an interior-sprung mattress regularly?

Yes, in order to prevent all the wear falling on certain sets of springs. Turn once every two or three weeks.

Are spiral springs better than woven ones for a bed?

Yes, but they are more expensive. If you do choose a woven one see that there is a means of tightening up if necessary, otherwise it is likely to sag after a few years' use.

What is the advantage of a box spring over a coil spring mattress?

The box spring is encased in fabric and the coil spring is uncovered.

What are the advantages of a rubber mattress?

These mattresses are made from Latex foam rubber and consequently wear extremely well and are especially resilient. They need no turning but it is advisable to change them from end to end. Some people find them a little warm during the summer months. They are more hygienic for invalids.

I am tall and want an extra long bed of special size. Can you tell me where I can find this?

Call in, or write to, the London Bedding Centre at Knightsbridge, London, S.W.1, and I believe they will be able to help you. This firm specialises in beds of all types and sizes.

Which is the best pillow—one filled with down or feathers?

Down is the most expensive filling and it is the softest. A mixture of down and feathers give a fairly soft pillow which is cooler to sleep on. The choice depends upon what sort of pillow you are looking for—medium-soft or very soft!

I have had the misfortune to buy a pair of sheets stated by the manufacturers to be "double-bed size" and they are much too small for my normal-sized double bed. How can I avoid this happening again?

These vague terms of double and single bed sizes are misleading because they vary considerably. It is advisable to insist on "large double bed" size or "large single bed" size, or better still, to measure your bed and discover the size of sheet you need. Measure the mattress of your bed allowing plenty of tuck-in at the foot, head, and sides, and check these measurements with those of the sheets before you buy them.

This kind of thing happens also when buying blankets so it is as well to check the size you want before buying. Allow for the thickness of the mattress plus 8-ins. at each side for a comfortable tuck-in, but the blanket need not be as long as the sheet because the very deep turn at the pillow is not necessary; allow enough to tuck in at the foot end and to turn over at the pillow end.

What are the usual sizes for bedcovers, down quilts and cot covers?

Bedcovers are 100 inches long and 70 or 80 inches wide for single beds and 90 inches wide for double beds. Down quilts are 6 ft. by 4 ft. wide and 6 ft. by 5 ft. wide. Cot quilts are usually 3 ft. by 2 ft. wide and 3 ft. 6 ins. by 2 ft. 6 ins. wide. Beware! Single bed sizes are often made shorter than double bed sizes—a crazy practice but a general one.

Does it matter whether a down quilt is filled with down or feathers?

Yes, because feathers are inclined to work their way through the cover and become a nuisance. Down is best.

How can I retain the lovely full appearance of my new down quilt?

By periodically giving it a very gentle shaking and patting with the hand to break up the little heaps of down inside.

Do you recommend a plain or patterned bedspread?

Because bedspreads occupy a relatively large area of the room I prefer a plain bedspread to a patterned one and in the dominant colour in the room. If you have a patterned bedspread the carpet, walls and curtains must be severely plain or it looks fussy.

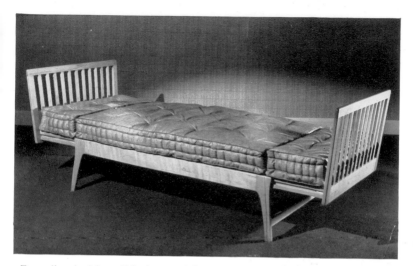

Extending bed in polished natural beech, 2 ft. 6 ins. wide and 4 ft. 6 ins. when closed, extends to 5 ft. 3 ins. or 6 ft. 3 ins. Complete with a 3-piece mattress set. From Heals.

Printed Irish linen furnishing fabrics designed by four Dublin painters and presented by John McGuire Ltd., through Hille of London Ltd.

PLATE 1

Three examples of contemporary electric lighting fittings by G.E.C. and (*bottom right*) the Tilley paraffin pressure table lamps which burn for 12 hours on 1½ pints paraffin.

PLATE 2

This G.E.C. baby alarm super-imposes the faintest cry or whimper over a radio programme being transmitted in another room.

The "Derek" folding high chair made of tubular steel which clips on to the back of any household chair or car seat.

PLATE 3

"Two Singles—One Double" Divan. It consists of two single divans which can be linked together with a zip fastener on the mattress making a 5 ft. 6 ins. double divan. The oval Divan (*inset left*) is designed for luxury. It is 6 ft. 6 ins. by 5 ft. and has a pocketed spring interior mattress mounted on a spring edge base. All from the London Bedding Centre.

PLATE 4

UPHOLSTERY

Are there any guiding rules as regards upholstery for contemporary furniture?

The colour and texture of the wood should be considered as well as the design of the furniture. For example, lacquered woods, walnut, mahogany, etc., need an elegant, sophisticated fabric, while bleached or natural oak, being coarse-grained and tough, can take a heavy, knobbly fabric of the tweedy type with good grace. With plain furniture, patterned fabrics look well. But if the furniture is extensively carved or decorated, a plain fabric should be chosen because the wood should be the focal point, and not the fabric.

Choose plain or small designs for small items of furniture, large patterned fabrics for large furniture. Be guided also by the size of the room when considering size of pattern. Washability and cleanability should also be considered. Very light and very dark colours are harder to keep clean because they show the dirt more quickly than medium shades.

Can you tell me how to measure a chair for loose covers?

Take away the cushion. Measure the chair from the floor at the back and down the front to the edge of the seat. Add 4-ins. for tuck-in where back and seat meet. Next, measure from the front edge of the arm to the floor. Add twice the measurement from floor across the arm to edge of seat and add 4-ins. for tuck-in and 1-inch for each seam allowance. Measure the cushion separately allowing 1-inch on all sides for seams.

For a flounce, add ¾-in. to the width you choose for seam and 1½-ins. for hem. For a gathered skirt, add one or two times the measurement around the chair for fullness. For a box-pleated skirt allow three times the measurement around the chair.

Pin the fabric, pattern upwards, where necessary, wrong side up over each section of the chair and cut the material carefully where necessary. Work the material into small darts over the curved section of the top of the chair. Allow 4-ins. tuck-in fold at seat edge of back and arms. Then remove the cover and insert cording before stitching. Fasten at the back on the left side with a zip fastener or snap tape.

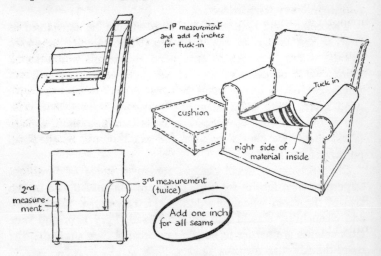

1st measurement and add 4 inches for tuck-in

Tuck in

cushion

right side of material inside

2nd measurement.

3rd measurement (twice)

Add one inch for all seams

Your advice on cleaning badly soiled upholstery, please

Providing the upholstery is of a washable sort, you can clean it with a solution of good quality soapless cleanser. Work on a small area at a time, and avoid saturating it; use a soft brush to work up the lather and rinse each patch as you clean it with a cloth wrung out in fresh water. Pat as dry as possible. Leave to dry either out of doors or near an open window. For less badly stained upholstery you could use a grease solvent like benzene or carbon tetrachloride—but avoid using in a room where there is a fire because it is inflammable.

What can I do to stretch loose covers which have shrunk in the wash and no longer fit the chairs?

Damp them all over, thoroughly. Then leave them rolled in a towel for a couple of hours. The covers should then be in a "stretchable" condition and a warm iron will remove traces of crumpling when you get the covers on the chairs.

I am attracted to a large-patterned fabric for my living-

room curtains but the room is small. Do you think the big-pattern will make it look still smaller?

Yes! Avoid big patterns in a small room. If your carpet and upholstered furniture are plain choose either a small neat pattern or, if your carpet and upholstery are patterned choose a plain material. Plain materials always give the impression of added size to a room.

CURTAINS

Can brocade curtains be washed successfully at home?

Some brocades may be washed at home but it is always safer to send them to the cleaners for dry cleaning. In between cleanings they can be freshened by rubbing over with a soft cloth moistened with carbon tetrachloride.

Plastic curtains appear difficult to sew—I never have much success with mine. What is the secret?

A little french chalk or talcum powder sprinkled between the layers of plastic, strong cotton and long loose stitches. Avoid deep hems because these do not lie flat ; finish raw edges by turning them over and binding with tape.

Is it necessary to have bed-covers and curtains of the same material?

Certainly not! But this is the modern trend. In this case the down quilt is placed under the bed-cover. If you have a down quilt and bedspread of matching material the quilt looks best on top of the bedspread during the day.

How much material do I need to recover an eiderdown— top only?

I assume this is double-bed size for which you will need between $4\frac{1}{3}$ and $4\frac{1}{2}$ yards of 36-inch fabric. Cut the material for the centre panel and stitch according to design after well tacking. Then cut the borders, mitre the corners and stitch inside edge, and slip-stitch to the edge of eiderdown.

Your guidance, please, on estimating the amount of

material I need for new curtains. How do you measure accurately so that you have enough, but not too much material?

Measure each window very carefully. To the actual length of each curtain add 6 to 7 inches of material—about 1 inch for turning underneath the gathering tape, 2 to 3 inches for the frill at the top and about 3 inches for the bottom hem. Double the total width of the window when allowing for the width of material, and allow 5 to 6 inches extra for overlap in the middle. This will allow the curtains to hang in attractive folds without skimpiness.

Allow approximately twice the width of the window for the valance frills; when deciding the depth of material, allow 2 to 3 inches for the hem and plenty of material for heading.

If you are lining your curtains remember that the width of lining materials are often different to those of the curtains; allow for this.

When hand-sewing the lining to a curtain I have difficulty in preventing the tacking stitches from going through to the right side of the curtain.

Slide a narrow piece of cardboard between the curtain and the lining, moving it as you go along and you will find it will solve this difficulty.

I don't know how to make or hang frilled cross-drape curtains. Can you instruct me?

You can buy ninon ready frilled then you need only hem the lower edge and make a slot for the rod or expanding curtain wire at the top. It is more satisfactory to use two rods or lengths of curtain wire, one for each curtain, but you can if you wish, use only one rod or wire and join the curtains at the top.

I have two difficult windows to curtain. One is too high and narrow and the other too low and wide. What sort of curtaining do you advise?

The high narrow window will look wider if you carry the curtain and pelmet rail 9 to 12 ins. beyond the actual window frame on either side. Curtains can then be drawn right back in the daytime to admit plenty of light. Choose a fabric with a horizontal stripe to give an impression of extra width.

For the low wide window I suggest a vertical striped material

with the curtains hanging to the ground. Have a narrow pelmet set *above* the window frame so that the hemline just covers the edge of the upper framework. Or the pelmet may be omitted.

I am thinking of sending some thick woven curtains to the cleaners and hope they will be able to remove light streaks which have appeared on the inside next to the win-

dows. **Do you think they will be able to get rid of them? If not, can I have the curtains dyed?**

The cleaners will not be able to remove the streaks in your curtains because, most likely, these have been caused by the sun which has faded the material when the curtains have been pulled back in the daytime. There is a danger, too, that the sun will have rotted the material that has faded and it may disintegrate during the cleaning process; this danger would be increased by dyeing because of the high temperatures necessary to fix the dye. If you are unprepared to take these risks you can clean the curtains yourself at home with carbon tetrachloride and line them to hide the faded streaks.

FLOORING

I am told there is a way of giving a dusty concrete floor a hard, waterproof surface. What is it?

Sweep up all the dust and wash over with hot water and soda—never use soap on a concrete floor. Dissolve 1 lb. waterglass in 1 gallon of warm water and swab this mixture all over the floor letting the concrete absorb just as much as it will. When absorption is complete, but before the floor is quite dry, apply a second coating again letting the concrete absorb as much as it will. Then leave to dry. You may be troubled with white patches for a day or two but these will soon disappear and you will have a waterproof, dust-free floor which you can polish in the usual way if you want.

Can I lay linoleum on a cement floor?

Yes, providing this is quite even and dry. It is necessary to have a good quality underlay stuck down with a special sealer or you can stick down your linoleum with a waterproof sealer like "Synthaprufe".

Please name suitable coverings for a stone floor.

You could apply a floor paint and then keep it polished if you wish. Alternatively, linoleum could be used, provided the floor is level and dry; you need a suitable underlay or the linoleum can be stuck down with a special waterproof adhesive.

Do you consider it worth while levelling an uneven stone floor?

If you wish to cover the floor in any way this is essential: you could float on to it a bed of $\frac{3}{4}$ to 1 inch asphalt in cement which would provide a level and satisfactory surface.

Can a cement floor be coloured once it is laid?

Yes! There are special paints on the market which the handyman can apply. "Cementone" is one of these and a variety of colours are available.

Is there any way of cutting down the labour involved in cleaning quarry tiles and cement floors?

Yes! They can be sealed with a rubber-based floor paint or a special tile paint to give a more easily cleaned surface. The paint will need renewing periodically and it is advisable to protect the main passage-ways with mats. It is essential to remove all trace of grease before applying the paint, and to give the paint sufficient time to dry before it is walked upon.

Is it wrong to wash linoleum each week?

Yes, because constant washing removes the oil from the linoleum and opens the pores; the linoleum becomes more absorbent to dirt and is harder to keep clean. Regular polishing is much more satisfactory, because it feeds and keeps it flexible.

What are the main considerations to note when choosing a flooring for the bathroom?

First, it should be easy to keep clean and not damaged by moisture; second, it should be warm to the feet. I recommend linoleum, plastic in sheet or tile form and rubber.

Is it necessary to buy an underlay for linoleum?

It is not essential but it will considerably lengthen the life of the linoleum and also make the floor warmer and more resilient. Special underlays are sold for this purpose; one type, a thick paper, is very inexpensive.

Is there any advantage in sticking down linoleum in a kitchen?

Sheet linoleum wears longer when it is stuck down and linoleum tiles must be stuck down to keep in position. When laid over cement it is important to have a waterproof underlay or to stick it down with a waterproof sealer like "Synthaprufe".

Can a floor seal be applied to linoleum to give a permanent gloss? If so, what sort of preparation is necessary?

A floor seal, such as the Bourne Seal, can be successfully applied to linoleum. Remove all dirt and rub all over with spirits of turpentine to remove all wax. If dirt still remains on the linoleum rub the affected parts with steel wool dipped in turpentine. See that the edges of the linoleum are firmly attached before treating with one or two coats of floor seal. Further coats can be applied until the necessary gloss is obtained. It will be necessary to repaint the linoleum with floor seal periodically.

What sort of flooring do you recommend for a kitchen?

In a kitchen you need a floor that is resistant to heat and grease, non-slippery and easy to clean. The PVC plastic floorings can be laid over cement, and you can buy them in tile or sheet form. Quarry tiles or cement floors are hardwearing so long as they are sealed to overcome their porosity, with a rubber-based floor paint or a special tile paint. Good quality linoleum is warmer than the other types of flooring. When laid over cement it should have a waterproof underlay or be stuck down with a waterproof sealer. It can be bought in sheet or tile form. Plain colours show footmarks more than marbled or all-over designs. Rubber can also be used in a kitchen.

What is the best way to clean plastic flooring?

Mop over in the usual way with soap and water, then use a water-wax emulsion such as those made by Furmoto, Goddards and Ronuk. Floor seals should not be used on plastic unless specially prepared for the job.

What is your opinion on cork flooring?

Compressed cork and cork tiles are quiet, easy to keep clean and they are ideal for the bathroom, hall, etc. Cork linoleum and cork carpet have a dull rough surface which is absorbent and therefore difficult to clean.

Ours is a composition floor and my worry is to know how to remove black marks from it.

Try steel wool; this generally is successful. Polish in the usual way after removing the marks.

Dirt has become badly ingrained in a wood block floor of a house I have just bought. Is there any way of renovating the floor?

E

It will be necessary for the floor to be sanded down and then polished with a polishing machine. There are several firms who specialise in this sort of work and I suggest you get the job done before you move into the house.

The castors of my easy chairs have made deep black marks in the linoleum surrounds. Can they be removed?

Rub the marks with steel wool moistened with turps till the black marks are removed then polish in the usual way. There is not very much you can do to remove the hollows.

Is it true that a new type of furniture castor really does prevent castor marks on the floor?

They help considerably to prevent marks on the floor and consist of a plastic dome disc with two cotter pins mounted in it by a ball and socket; these allow the castors to swivel round. They can be fitted by the handyman. Armstrongs Furniture Rests are among those I have tested with satisfactory results.

It is impossible to fill up the gaps between the floorboards of my lounge which is exceptionally large. Can you recommend an inexpensive all-over treatment to prevent draughts?

You could cover it with sheets of $\frac{5}{16}$-inch, $\frac{3}{8}$-inch or $\frac{1}{2}$-inch insulating fibre building board, which costs a few pence a square foot. This makes a first-class underlay for a carpet or linoleum.

Is there any way of removing rubber heel and sole marks from linoleum?

Yes! Rub with a soft cloth moistened with turpentine, or turpentine substitute.

How can I remove small spots of paint from the windows and floors after decorating?

Rub with fine steel wool then clean and polish in the usual way.

Is there a way of removing cement marks from a tiled floor without harming the tiles?

Apply a solution of hydrochloric acid—1 part acid to 6 parts water, and rinse off in a minute or so with clean fresh water.

Repeat if necessary. This acid is very poisonous and powerful in action and great care is needed in its use.

CARPETS

Do you recommend the "needleloom" carpet that is being advertised such a lot?

This depends for which room you intend to use it. It is quite serviceable in a bedroom where it is unlikely to get a lot of hard wear, but I cannot recommend it for a living-room or a hall where there is constant wear and tear. The fact that these carpets are rubber backed and do not need a separate underlay is an advantage and the prices are reasonable. Unfortunately, the colours are not very imaginative as yet.

I believe carpets and rugs can be moth-proofed; is this permanent?

No, it must be renewed every few years and after each washing. The cost is estimated by the square yard, and the job is undertaken by many of the established firms of cleaners and dyers. When the moth-proofing is done during manufacture it is more or less permanent.

What is the most economical width for wall-to-wall carpeting?

This depends on the size of the room. If you find that 27-in. carpet can be used without waste this is recommended because it is so easily adjustable for different sized rooms if you move houses and can be turned round if it wears thin in patches later on.

I cannot decide whether to buy a plain or patterned carpet.

Be guided by the size of your room and the type of furniture and upholstery that you have. A patterned carpet is practical only when the upholstery and walls are in plain colours, but plain carpets can be used with either plain or patterned walls, upholstery and fittings. Again, a patterned carpet detracts from the size of the room while a plain carpet gives the visual impression of extra size.

We are finding great difficulty in choosing the colour for our sitting-room carpet. What should be the deciding factors?

Do you want the carpet to set the dominant colour of the room or be in a subsidiary and complimentary colour? This is the first question to settle. If you want your carpet to take the main colour for the room it should be a very definite colour of character, and different from the walls, ceiling and upholstery. If the carpet is to be part of the background for your main colour which may be set by your curtains, upholstery or decorations, then the carpet should be in a complimentary shade of the dominant colour, or in a different but complimentary colour.

Can you advise me on the "pros" and "cons" of a fitted carpet against one of the stock size carpets that leave a border?

The stock-size carpets that leave a border all round reduce the apparent size of the room, and if the carpets themselves have a border, the apparent size is reduced even more. Against this, the price of stock-size carpets is lower than that of fitted carpets, and they are comparatively easy to lay and take up because much of the heavy furniture, usually placed round the walls, is only partly resting on the carpet, if at all.

As well as giving an appearance of additional size to a room, a fitted carpet is often considerably warmer and looks more comfortable and luxurious; it is important to have it moth-proofed because moths are apt to invade the fitted carpets at the edges next to the skirting boards. If bought in 27-in. widths the lengths can be switched round when patches show wear in later years.

Is it true that when you buy an inexpensive carpet it is best to buy a plain one because you are more likely to get value for money?

It is true to say that in a plain carpet or rug all the money goes into the product; there are no expensive designs, no special small-quantity dyeing of the yarns, and new loom adjustments to be made, all of which have to be paid for by the customer buying a patterned carpet or rug. On the other hand, you may be prepared to pay a few shillings more to have a pattern which can make all the difference to the appearance of a room.

Is it always advisable to buy the top-priced carpet or rug when you want to ensure making a good "buy"?

Not really. It all depends where you want to use the carpet or rug and how much wear and tear it is likely to receive. Sometimes where there is a young family it is better to get a medium-priced carpet that will last six or seven years till the family is older, then invest in a top-grade carpet. It all depends on individual circumstances.

Is it necessary to have a felt underlay for a carpet laid on wood?

Yes, because it reduces the wear and tear on the carpet considerably. It also gives a springy, luxurious feel to even quite a thin carpet when you walk over it.

How can you tell if a rug or carpet is of good quality?

By the height of the pile, the closeness of the pile or weave, and the quality of the yarn and backing.

Check the pile comparing different grades of carpet side by side. High pile is not, by itself, an indication of good quality and it must be combined with a close pile or weave if it is to wear well. It is difficult for a customer to judge the quality of the yarn, and reliance must be placed on the salesman's recommendations and the name of the manufacturer; always choose a product from a reputable factory.

I want a carpet that will not need a lot of care and attention, and will not show the dirt.

Choose a carpet of middle to high-grade with a two-tone pattern, neither too light nor too dark.

I intend to cut the best pieces from a carpet we are replacing with a new one and use them as rugs. Is there an easy way to bind the edges?

The rubber latex and synthetic plastic adhesives like "Copydex" have made the task of carpet binding very much easier and quicker. Trim back the pile from the edge to be bound, tuck the fibres underneath and apply a layer of adhesive. Then apply adhesive to a piece of hessian binding cut to the right length and press this down on to the fibres very firmly. Pile heavy books or other weighty objects on top and leave for 7 to 8 hours to dry.

The colours in my Persian carpet have faded through sun and age. Can these be restored?

It is unlikely that the colours can be completely restored but you can freshen them considerably by rubbing the carpet all over with a pad of soft material wrung out in ammonia and warm water—1 tablespoonful of ammonia to 1 pint warm water. Leave to dry completely before walking over it.

Which wears best—an Axminster or Wilton carpet?

Both are cut-pile carpets made from wool or worsted yarn worked into a canvas backing. The Axminster has a little longer and less closely woven pile than the Wilton type of carpet and for this reason it does not wear quite so long.

I am told it would be wrong to use my vacuum cleaner on my new carpet which is shedding a great deal of fluff that is a nuisance. What do you suggest?

You are right, it is unwise to use an electric vacuum cleaner on a new carpet till the pile has had time to settle. Brush lightly with a long handled brush to get rid of the fluff and any dust or threads, etc., or use a carpet sweeper for the job. You can begin to use the vacuum cleaner as soon as the carpet stops shedding fluff.

I have coconut matting in my kitchen; is there any way to clean it?

Yes! Scrub with soapy water, rinse in cold water to which a little salt has been added and spread out on the lawn to dry. Choose a dry day for the job, and see the grass is dry before you spread out the matting; if it is advisable to spread newspapers over the grass before laying the mat out.

I shampooed my carpet and it seems I must have put

back the furniture before the carpet was dry because the chair castors have left ugly rusty marks on the carpet and the furniture legs have dug deep into the pile and left hollows in the pile.

You can try shampooing the marked parts of your carpet again, rubbing gently with a soft nail brush—this will brush up the pile if you go against it, and help to loosen the rust marks. Leave to dry thoroughly before putting back any of your furniture.

KITCHEN EQUIPMENT

Is there any place in London where I can go and see the latest equipment and appliances for the home?

Yes, the Building Centre, Store Street, off Tottenham Court Road, London, W.1. You can obtain details of all exhibits but the Centre does not undertake to recommend products. This is a permanent exhibition, admission is free, and special displays are held from time to time. A similar exhibition is established in Edinburgh.

What are the chief factors to consider when choosing a cooker?

First, choose the size of oven you will need: as a safe guide decide upon the biggest turkey you are likely to want to cook in it at Christmas and find out if the cookers you like will accommodate this and, next, consider the hob; for a family of 4 to 6 people you will need two boiling plates and a grill boiler. For a family of 2 to 4 people you could probably manage on one boiling plate and a grill boiler.

I have been searching unsuccessfully for a solid fuel cooker which will supply both hot water for domestic use and for two small radiators. Can you help me?

Providing the radiators are placed near the boiler and therefore avoid a long pipe line, the Triplex "V" and "W" models would be suitable. And as an alternative I can recommend the new Sunbeam "Superior" cooker. The important thing is to cut down pipe line and not to open the fire doors more than necessary because every bit of heat radiated into the kitchen through the open fire doors is so much less for the water!

I am told I ought to have radiant boiling plates fitted to my electric cooker. How do they differ from the solid boiling plates and why are they recommended?

The radiant boiling plate looks like a red hot spiral; it heats up

"New World" Eighty-four gas cooker made by Radiation with cantilever hob and flue outlet in splashback.

New "Crusader" gas cooker by General Gas Appliances has a specially designed flat-top hot plate.

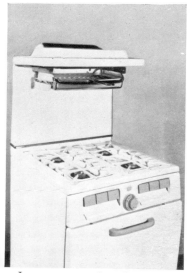

Luxury gas cooker "Renown Five" (*left*) has a twin eye-level grill with automatic ignition. Falco "Royal" electric cooker (*right*), with controls grouped on the back panel and large enclosed grill. The automatic timer enables a prepared meal to be cooked at any required time when the housewife is absent from the kitchen or home. PLATE 5

The "Yorkseal" heat retention solid fuel cooker burns continuously, supplies hot water for domestic use and keeps the kitchen warm with low fuel consumption.

The BNE C.90 electric cooker is spacious and good-looking with a commendable absence of grooves which would make cleaning difficult.

The "Aga" solid fuel cooker is heavily insulated and automatically controlled. Fuel consumption is comparatively low and efficiency is high.

This 3 cu. ft. G.E.C. electric refrigerator is claimed to be sufficiently well lagged to enable it to be placed next to a cooker without efficiency being impaired.

PLATE 6

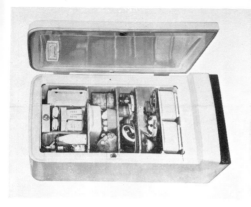

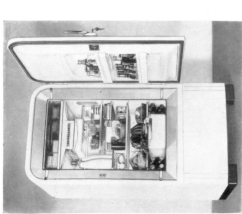

The 5 cu. ft. "Electrolux" refrigerator (*top left*) which will operate equally well by gas, electricity or oil. A full-width frozen storage compartment and bottle storage racks in the door are among its special features.

The 1½ cu. ft. "Astral" refrigerator (*top centre*) operates by gas, electricity or oil. There is an unchilled storage locker at the bottom for canned foods, jams, sauces, etc.

The 7 cu. ft. "Coldrator" electric refrigerator (*top right*) incorporates a compartment known as a "Buttador" in the door of the refrigerator where butter may be stored for short periods at room temperature ready for spreading.

A cold drawer where food may be chilled quickly, and a full-width freezer to accommodate up to 30 lb. of frozen packet food at safe temperature from 1 to 2 weeks, are features of this 8 cu. ft. "English Electric" refrigerator (*bottom right*).

PLATE 7

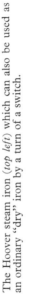

The Hoover steam iron (*top left*) which can also be used as an ordinary "dry" iron by a turn of a switch.

G.E.C. claim this "Bride's" iron (*top centre*), weighing only 2⅛ lb., to be the lightest full-size domestic iron on the market. It is fitted with automatic temperature control for various fabrics.

The Tilley paraffin pressure domestic iron (*top right*), without wires or flexes, and with complete heat control. It burns for 4 hours on one-third pint of paraffin.

The Kenwood electric Chef (*bottom left*) prepares most types of food easily and efficiently.

The electric "Xpelair" draught-proof stale air extractor (*bottom right*) is good for getting rid of condensation and cooking smells in a kitchen. It can be installed easily into window glass and partitions.

PLATE 8

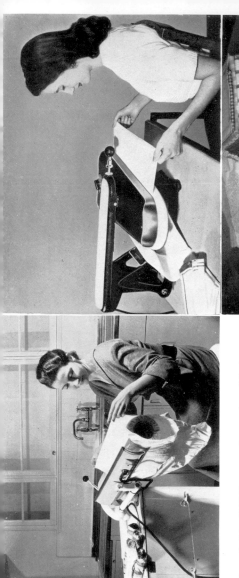

The roller of this G.E.C. rotary ironer (*top left*) has an open end which can be inserted into the shoulders of garments, sleeves and cuffs.

The Parnall "Ezy-Press" ironer (*top right*) is designed on the flat-press principle. Frills, collars, etc., can be ironed by drawing them over the wide heated brim of the ironing plate.

The "Phantom" gas-heated iron set (*bottom right*). The irons are used as a pair, one being heated on the heating unit and then transferred to the trivet for use while the second iron is heating. There is no flex to restrict the use of the iron. Can be operated with "town" or bottled gas.

PLATE 9

The electric "Wastemaster" which is fitted below the sink outlet, and shreds all normal kitchen waste into tiny pieces and flushes them down the drain.

The "Dishmaster" electric dishwasher which washes, rinses and dries in a few minutes at the touch of a dial. The whole operation is entirely automatic.

The Hoover, Mark I, washing machine with table top and plinth base, empties automatically by means of a pump and has a hand-operated wringer.

This "English Electric" washing machine has a 3 k.w. immersion heater fitted in the base of the tub, and a power-operated wringer. A rotary ironing attachment is interchangeable with the wringer.

PLATE 10

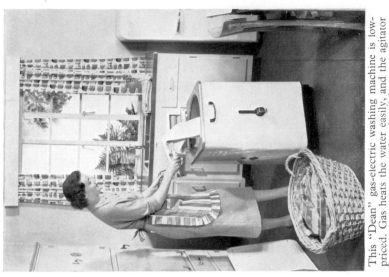

This "Dean" gas-electric washing machine is low-priced. Gas heats the water easily, and the agitator is operated by electricity.

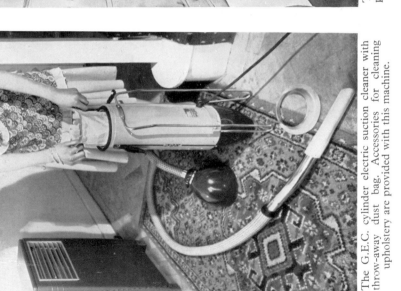

The G.E.C. cylinder electric suction cleaner with throw-away dust bag. Accessories for cleaning upholstery are provided with this machine.

PLATE 11

All surfaces of this kitchen including the work surfaces and dinette table, and the cupboard doors and wall under the window, are veneered with linette "Formica".

The new Hoover "Junior" electric suction cleaner (*bottom left*), with cleaning tools for "above the floor" purposes.

The Hoover "Dustette" (*bottom centre*). The Hoover electric polisher and scrubber (*bottom right*).

PLATE 12

quickly and glows red when full on. The solid flat metal disc-type of hot-plate is slower to heat up and to lose heat and remains black even when hot. The two types are interchangeable in post-war cookers.

What is a Simmerstat switch and what does it do?

This is a new type of variable electric switch for electric boiling plates and grill-boilers which enables you to regulate the heat to whatever strength you like from a quick boil down to a gentle simmer.

Are ground base pans essential with the radiant type of electric hot-plate?

No! A thinner type of pan is an advantage with a radiant hot-plate, but ground base pans are necessary for solid hot-plates in order to make all-over contact with the hot-plate and save both fuel and time.

The baking tin supplied with my small gas cooker is quite a lot smaller than the oven. Is there any reason why I should not use a bigger tin the size of the oven shelves?

Yes! A tin which just fitted the oven shelves would prevent the heat circulating and result in uneven cooking of the food in the oven. This is why the baking tins should always be slightly smaller than the oven shelves.

What is the best work surface in a kitchen?

Laminated plastics, "Formica" and "Wareite", are excellent. They are heat and acid-resisting and can be put on existing tables and work tops so long as the surface is level. Good quality enamel is a reliable alternative, and stainless steel gives an extremely durable though expensive surface.

What is your opinion of the upright and cylinder electric suction cleaners? Which is best?

Both types do a good job and the choice should depend on individual circumstances. The upright cleaners are ideal for houses with carpeted rooms, especially if these rooms are large; the cylinder cleaners are suited for general cleaning, and particularly for the cleaning of rugs, also carpets, in places where space is very restricted, such as small flats.

What are the chief uses of an electric duster?

These electric "dusters" are most useful for cleaning stair carpets and upholstery and mattresses, also car upholstery, because they are so manageable. They should be regarded as an auxiliary to the vacuum cleaner.

Are non-electric suction cleaners efficient?

Yes, so long as you remember they are non-electric and therefore cannot be expected to operate in quite the same way as electric cleaners. It is important to remember that a good swinging motion is necessary with these cleaners and so they are the most efficient over large carpeted areas.

I have only a limited area of floor to polish but as I am unable to kneel I want to buy a floor polisher. I do not feel it is worth while buying an electric polisher for such a small area and so I would appreciate your opinion as to whether the non-electric polishers are any good.

They are quite efficient and those that incorporate an automatic device for spreading the wax are especially good for a small area such as your own. The "Daz" is one polisher of this type that I have found satisfactory.

Are food mixers worth buying?

This depends entirely upon the size of your family and how much cooking you do. If there are only one or two in family and you seldom bake cakes, make puddings, soufflés, and so on, then a food mixer will not be much good to you. If you have a large family and cook something of this type once or twice a week, or even more often, a food mixer of the Kenwood class will be a boon. You will find the attachments for mincing and chopping, grating, potato peeling, juice extracting, slicing, mixing dough, etc., invaluable, too.

Is there a clothes washing machine which will boil the water?

There are a number of washing machines which heat their own water and you should choose one of these; the "Parnall", "Swirlux", "English Electric", "Servis", etc., are a few of these, operated by electricity, and the gas-heated models include the Morley and the Dean.

Which are the machines which will partly dry the clothes after they have been washed?

The "Bendix" is a good machine of this type, and the "Thor" is another you might like to see: both spin-dry the clothes.

I am told there is a combined clothes and dish-washer but I am unable to trace it.

The "Thor Automagic" spin dry washer is the machine you are looking for. Any "Thor" dealer will supply you. You buy the clothes washer and the dish-washing unit is an optional extra.

Which are the flat press type domestic ironers?

At a time of going to press there are two—the "Hotpoint" and the "Ezy-Press". Both operate on the flat-press principle and have a wide heated brim round which frilly garments, collars, etc., may be pressed to iron out the creases.

Why don't the manufacturers produce irons for left-handed users?

They do! Some irons already on the market have a swivelling flex outlet at the back and some have both right- and left-hand thumb rests so that they can be used with ease by both right- and left-handed people.

How should one choose between a lightweight and a heavyweight electric iron?

This depends partly on personal preference and partly on the electric loading of the iron. A lightweight iron of relatively high loading, 750 to 1,000 watts will be satisfactory for almost all types of work but care must be taken to avoid scorching when operating at full heat. Lightweight irons of this loading are excellent for the quick ironer. For a slower ironer 600 to 750 watts loading and a heavier iron will be found more satisfactory in most cases.

How can the sole-plate of an electric iron be cleaned?

It can be rubbed with a damp cloth and occasionally when further cleaning is required, the sole-plate can be cleaned with silver plate polish.

Do you recommend gas irons?

Personally, I prefer irons provided with a gas-heated stand rather than the gas-heated irons because this way you avoid the piping which is apt to get in the way when ironing. The gas-heated stands are provided with two irons so that one iron is heated while the other is being used. They are quite efficient, reliable and absolutely safe under normal conditions, but they are not so convenient as the thermostatically controlled electric irons.

Are the electric ironing machines worth buying for the small household? If so can you tell me more about them?

It is worthwhile investing in an electric ironing machine if you launder bedlinen, tablecloths, towels and many other flat articles at home. Although the clothes washer helps a lot to cut down wash-day labour, it still leaves the equally tiring job of ironing still to be tackled, and the electric ironers can save both time and energy.

The domestic machines are of two main types. One, the roller type, consists of a heated metal shoe that closes down on an automatic revolving padded roller on which laundry is arranged. The flat-press-ironer which can be used for both ironing and pressing clothes, is similar in design to the pressers you see in a dry-cleaning and pressing establishment; necklines and frills can be ironed on the flat ironer by drawing them against the broad rim of the heated shoe.

Most of the rotary ironers are designed to operate from the wringer power drive on individual washing machines; exceptions are the "Oprim" and the "Pressmatic", which operate independently. The flat press ironers operate independently from any convenient power point.

Factors to look for when considering the purchase of an electric ironing machine include:

Rotary Ironer: The speed at which the padded roller revolves; when too quick it is difficult to arrange the material quickly enough.

The size of roller: this should be quite large. When the ironer operates in conjunction with a clothes washer, test that the washer forms a sufficiently firm stand and cannot tip over when the heavy ironer is being used.

Flat Press Ironer: Check that the ironing surface is sufficiently large for your needs. That the operation is easy. For example, the "Hotpoint" is designed with two operating levers while the "Ezy-Press" has only one; it is up to you to decide which you find most easy to manipulate. Check that the heated shoe will remain in position over, for example, a folded sheet, and will not spring up directly the lever is released. This enables the user to relax often while ironing.

Would you advise me to buy an electric steam iron?

If you do a lot of pressing—suits, odd skirts, coats, etc., you will find the steam iron a boon because, with the exception of serge, a protective cloth need not be used over the material while ironing. You would also find it useful if you wash heavy linens at home because the steam iron makes damping down unnecessary. It can of course, be used as a dry iron too, just by switching a knob. If your ironing consists mainly of underwear and personal belongings, and you do not have need to press your clothes and those of your family, you would not find the steam iron such a big help over an ordinary electric iron with thermostatic heat control.

I read about an adjustable-height ironing board and an

adjustable height kitchen stool but I cannot trace them in the shops.

There are a number of ironing boards with two or three positions for the tall and short woman and the woman of average height; these heights allow also for standing and sitting heights which is most useful. The "Camyad" is one board I know well which is sturdily constructed of tubular steel. The "Floating Stool" which is adjusted merely by turning the padded seat clockwise or anti-clockwise, according to the height you want, has the additional advantage of specially designed springs which give a sideways as well as a backwards-and-forwards movement which cuts down fatigue when you are sat working—you may have seen it on TV Inventor's Club some time ago.

HEATING

Before deciding on the type of heating to install in my new house I want to find out comparative costs of the various heating methods.

This depends very much upon the efficiency as well as on the type of unit that you choose, and also on the quality of the fuel you burn. You can build up a fairly accurate picture on the following figures when you have ascertained the prices of the different fuels in your area. These figures are *approximate*.

Household coal and coke (for heating individual rooms): $\frac{2}{3}$ to 1 lb. per 2,000 cu. ft. of room space per hour.

Coke (for central heating): $\frac{3}{4}$ lb. per 2,000 cu. ft. room space per hour.

Gas: 34 cu. ft. per 2,000 cu. ft. room space per hour.

Electricity: 2 units (2,000 watts) per 2,000 cu. ft. room space per hour.

Oil: $\frac{1}{3}$ pint oil per 2,000 cu. ft. room space per hour.

I want information about the single heating unit that will warm a whole house by means of air ducts.

Radiation Ltd. have developed a unit which, as you suggest, will heat the whole house and provide domestic hot water from a single self-contained unit by applying the ducted air principle. The unit is thermostatically controlled and it can be operated either by solid fuel, or gas or oil. For a properly insulated house of 1,000 sq. ft. floor area, an average fuel consumption is approximately 4 tons of coal, coke, anthracite, etc., and this will maintain the whole house at 60 deg. F. at all times, the living room including dining space, at 67 deg. F. for 8 hours per day and the bedroom at 65 deg. F. for 4 hours per day as well as 50 deg. or more gals. per day of water at 140 deg. F. An extra 20 therms of gas is required for water heating in the summer when space heating is not required.

The temperature of each room to which warm air is ducted can be controlled thermostatically.

In the case of the gas-operated model, a consumption of 600 therms of gas annually in a properly insulated house with a floor area of 1,000 sq. ft. will maintain a temperature of 60 degs. F. at all times, living and dining space at 63 deg. F. for 8 hours per day. In addition 250 therms of gas will be needed to supply 250 gals. per week of water at 140 deg. F. at the tap. The domestic hot water can conveniently be provided by a "New World" gas circulator or a "Nautilus" coke boiler.

How much does it cost to install central heating?

This depends upon how compact the house is and the size of the radiators you choose. As a very rough estimate you can allow £25 to £30 per radiator, plus about £40 to £50 for the boiler and £30 for the "indirect" hot water cylinder. So to install central heating in an average size 3-bedroom home without any unusual features the cost is likely to be from £200 to £225 to give 5 radiators and 1 boiler. When central heating is installed in a house that is being built it would be cheaper. These figures do, of course, include not only the heating but the complete hot water system; they do not include special building work such as the provision of a brick chimney.

What are the ideal "background" temperatures for a living room and bedroom?

Ideally, the living room temperature should not fall below 58 deg. F. and the bedroom not below 52 deg. F. These are comfortable temperatures, too low for the room to feel stuffy but sufficiently high to prevent the dampness and chilliness that exists in rooms heated only when in use. This method of background heating for a room prevents the wastage of heat in warming up a room that has got really cold. These temperatures need topping up by separate appliances—a solid fuel open fire or stove for the living room, gas or electric fire for the bedrooms when the rooms are occupied. Because the rooms are already partially warmed much less heat is required than if the rooms were cold.

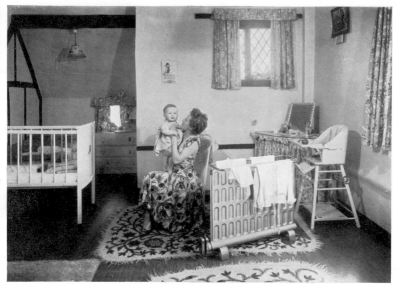

The "Dimplex" oil-filled electric radiators, which can be fitted with towel rails, are very suitable for use in the nursery.

Radiation and convected heat is provided by this "Berry" electric space heater with pre-set thermostat. The heating unit is totally enclosed and it is recommended for use in a nursery.

PLATE 13

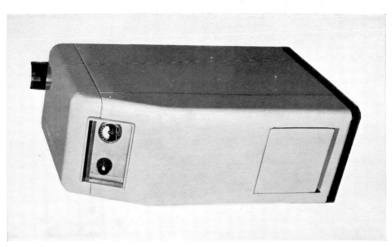
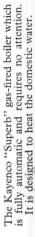

The Kayenco "Superb" gas-fired boiler which is fully automatic and requires no attention. It is designed to heat the domestic water.

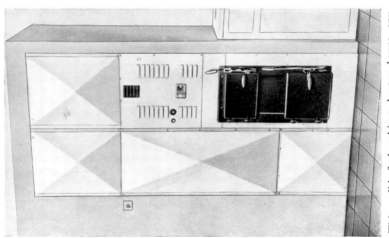

This solid fuel cabinet heater burns any domestic fuel and is the "core" of the radiation system of whole house warming by

PLATE 14

This neat looking heater burns oil most efficiently without smell.

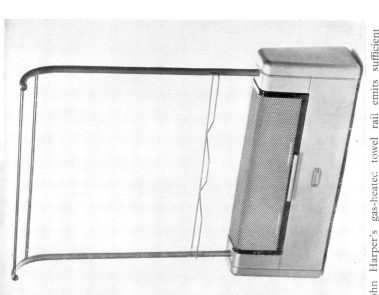

John Harper's gas-heated towel rail emits sufficient warmth to take the chilliness from the bathroom.

PLATE 15

An advantage of the Cannon K.12 portable gas fire is that it can be carried from one room to another and connected to an existing gas point.

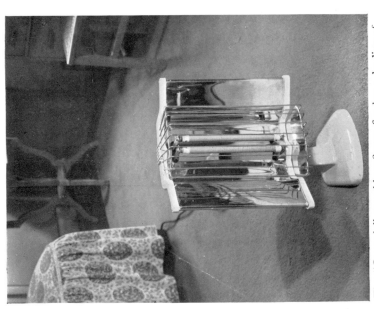

The "Cosy-glo" portable reflector fire has a loading of 2 k.w. and is designed to radiate heat evenly and give

PLATE 16

The "Parkray No. 1" stand-in convector fire (*left*) prevents wastage of heat up the chimney and heats a room 15 ft. by 13 ft. by 8 ft. 6 ins. on an average weekly consumption of only 1 cwt. of fuel. Radiant heat and convected warm air are provided by this unit. The Tilley paraffin pressure radiator (*centre*) which will burn for 12 hours on 1½ pints of paraffin, and is completely portable. The Main B.B.U. back boiler conversion unit (*right*) is a gas heater designed for use with the back boiler of an ordinary open grate. It will provide hot water in summer without a fire.

PLATE 17

The "Port Royal" convector radiant gas fire effects a considerable saving of gas as a result of its unique design. It radiates heat in all directions.

The C.P. portable screen gas fire has a heat output of a fixed fire and is designed to stand in the fireplace. It can easily be moved from one room to another.

PLATE 18

The "Rayburn" room heater has two openable fire doors. Heating is by convection as well as radiation and is continuous day and night.

The "Polkadot" fire fits most 16-in. fireplaces, is easy to instal, needs no sealing or fixing and looks good with contemporary furnishings.

PLATE 19

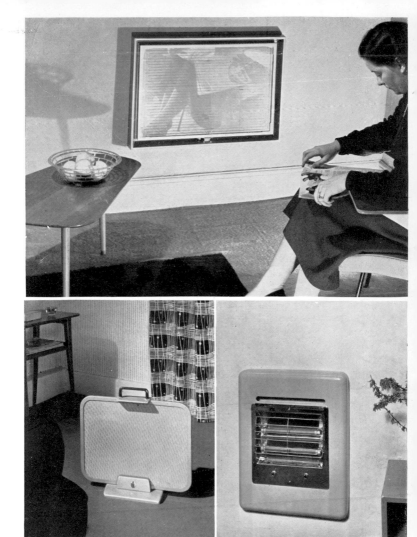

The "Thermovent" radiant glass "Thermopanel", with wall frame (*top*), designed to fit in with contemporary furnishings. Infra-red rays warm objects immediately and radiation begins within three minutes of switching on. The Morphy-Richards panel heater (*bottom left*) is particularly safe because the heating element is completely embedded and the low surface temperature prevents the possibility of burns. The "Solectra" panel fire (*bottom right*) has a loading of 2 k.w. and is fixed to the wall by four concealed screws. It is particularly suited to bedrooms.

PLATE 20

The "Windsor" gas-operated convector heater is ideal for heating the hall and for background heating of a living-room.

The convector gas fire FA/7 (*left*), made by the Ascot people, will provide radiant and convective heat in halls and corridors or living-rooms.

PLATE 21

The "Hurdapta" convector open fire combines the cosy appearance and comfort of an open fire with the economy and efficiency of a stove. It has a restricted throat, controlled by a damper, which prevents excessive ventilation and loss of heat up the chimney.

The "Redfyre 55" (*right*) continuous burning fire which will stay alight day and night all through the winter if required.

PLATE 22

The Crane 25A boiler for hot-water supply has an open-fire front and hotplate top. It will remain alight for 14–16 hours when burning coke; anthracite and other smokeless fuel may also be burnt.

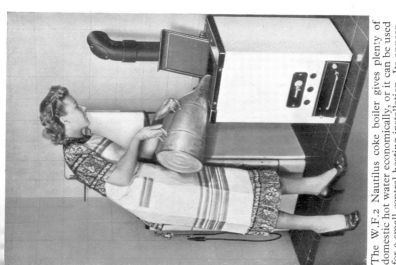

The W.F.2 Nautilus coke boiler gives plenty of domestic hot water economically, or it can be used for a small central heating installation. Its appearance is neat and attractive, and it is easy to clean.

PLATE 23

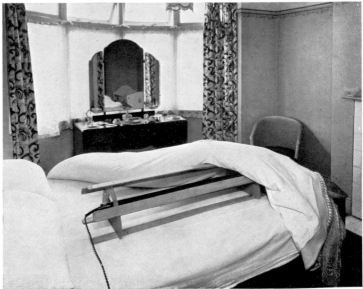

The "New Carlton" boiler (*top*) which burns solid fuels and provides domestic hot water and central heating. G.E.C. combined bed or cupboard heater (*bottom*) has a loading of 75 W. and reaches a maximum temperature of 120 degrees F. in about one hour when placed in bed with eiderdown and blanket covering.

PLATE 24

How much does it cost to provide central heating and domestic hot water by solid fuel boiler for a family of four in a 3-bedroom house?

This is a difficult question but experiments conducted by the Building Research Station show that at the time of going to press the approximate cost would be 13s. 6d. to 16s. 6d. weekly according to the size of the house, number of baths and the amount of hot water used, etc.

Is it possible to get a really efficient solid fuel boiler that if sufficiently insulated will not heat the kitchen in warm weather?

The "Agamatic" is one of the best insulated solid fuel boilers and radiates comparatively little heat into the kitchen.

Is it true that it is unwise to install a boiler with openable fire doors for central heating purposes?

This sort of boiler can be "opened" to sit by but the heat radiated into the kitchen is so much less for the hot water; the fire begins to die down when the front is opened. For this reason if you want to operate a fairly extensive central heating system I advise you to choose a closed type of boiler in preference to one with a drop-down front. One or two radiators with short pipe line and domestic hot water can be operated very satisfactorily from an open-fire boiler of the Crane 40A type.

Is it possible to get a really efficient solid fuel cooker that will not make the kitchen very hot in warm weather?

This type of unit is naturally rather warm to work by in warm weather but you can get very well insulated cookers like the "Esse" and the "Aga" which throw out the minimum of heat into the kitchen. But the kitchen is still warm in hot weather.

I would like to install central heating but I do not want to ruin the appearance of my home by having ugly pipes everywhere. Can the pipes be concealed?

Some exposed pipes are unavoidable without extensive and expensive alterations to the building, but if you employ a skilled heating engineer there should be few visible. It is always best to

F

have central heating put in during the building of the house because then most of the pipes can be concealed in the walls and under the floorboards, so that very little sign of the heating is visible except for the radiators and the boiler which can be pleasing in appearance.

I am keen to have central heating but we haven't a basement. Is it satisfactory to have a boiler installed in the kitchen?

This depends upon the sort of boiler you want to install. There is no reason at all why you should not put a solid fuel boiler in the kitchen; in fact it is an advantage to have it there because it provides a certain amount of warmth for the kitchen. Only in the case of an oil-fired boiler is it preferable to have it installed in a basement because of the need to prevent the slightest smell of oil getting into the house.

Is it possible to install a single solid fuel unit to heat the water for domestic use and provide adequate whole house heating, and also provide cooking facilities?

No! This is unsatisfactory. It is much better to buy a separate solid fuel unit to cope with extensive central heating and domestic hot water and either a solid fuel, electric or gas cooker.

What are the advantages of oil-fired and gas-fired boilers? Are there any disadvantages?

Oil-fired and gas-fired boilers are entirely automatic in operation. There is no stoking to be done and they do not need cleaning out. Labour and maintenance is therefore eliminated. Against this the cost of operating is much higher than that of solid fuel boilers; a gas-fired boiler can safely be installed in a kitchen without fear of any smell penetrating to the house, but an oil-fired boiler should be installed in a cellar to prevent the risk of the smell of oil getting into the house and an oil store is necessary.

Can any sort of fuel be burnt by solid fuel boilers and cookers?

All solid fuel units are found to operate better on some types of fuels better than others, and to get the best out of these units it is important to buy the type of fuel recommended by the manufacturers. If you are unsure ask the retailer from whom you bought the unit, or get into touch with the Coal Utilisation Council in London.

I have a large well insulated boiler in the kitchen to heat the water and provide a limited amount of central heating. The kitchen gets very cold in winter and I want to install a supplementary form of heating. What do you suggest?

If it is not possible to run an extra radiator off your heating system to warm the kitchen I suggest either electric tubular heaters, which can be mounted on the skirting singly, in pairs or in sets of three or more to operate at black heat most economically, *or* electric oil-filled radiators, *or* oil burning radiators *or* the electric or gas convectors. Since only a relatively small amount of heating is required running costs should be low.

How much time and labour is involved in stocking and attending a solid fuel boiler which supplies both water for domestic use and for central heating?

The Building Research Station proved in their recent experiments that the average time taken in tending the appliances including fetching fuel from store, cleaning out grates and stoves as well as refuelling them, was less than 10 minutes each day.

My solid fuel boiler heats the kitchen too much in summer and so I want to install an alternative method of water heating. What do you suggest?

There are several methods of combining a solid fuel boiler with another form of water-heating; they include a gas circulator, electric immersion heater, multi point gas water heater, electric storage heater and gas or electric sink heaters. When a gas circulator or electric immersion heater are connected to the hot water system, they can be thermostatically controlled so that if the fire in the boiler dies down and the water drops below a certain temperature, the circulator or immersion heater automatically comes into operation and heats the water to the predetermined temperature when it automatically cuts out. This is a great help in the cold weather and also on occasions when it is inconvenient to refuel the boiler at the normal times. In summer, the gas circulator or electric immersion heater operates in just the same way without the boiler; it is possible with an immersion heater to arrange during the day for only a few gallons of water in the tank to be heated and then when baths are required or wash day arrives, a second switch can be turned on and the remainder of water in the tank can be heated—two heaters are fitted to the tank.

Do you recommend that the hot-water storage tank and circulating pipes should be insulated? When this is done does it make the airing cupboard useless?

I do recommend it, most strongly! The heat loss through unlagged hot-water storage tank and circulating pipes can be considerable in the colder weather. Specially designed storage tank jackets and pipe lagging is sold by most ironmongers and hardware shops. When airing is to be done, a flap of the jacket can be turned back to allow a limited amount of heat to escape into the airing cupboard.

The heating engineers who are installing central heating say I should have the house insulated to preserve the heat. Is this necessary?

It is not essential but it ensures you get the full benefit of your heating. Roofs and sometimes walls, are lined with insulating materials; doors and windows are fitted with weather strips to prevent draughts and the floors are adequately covered to prevent draughts striking through the floorboards.

Do you recommend heating the water for domestic purposes by electricity? What types of heaters are available?

This is a highly efficient and labour-saving way of heating domestic water but it is more expensive than solid fuel. You can choose between the—

Self-contained storage heater to supply all the taps in the house, which consists of a heat-retaining cylinder with a water heating element (or elements) built in, which are made in various sizes; some have two heating elements—one to give plenty of hot water for ordinary use during the day, and a larger one which can be turned on for baths and wash-day.

The sink heater which is fitted on the wall near the sink or wash-basin and supplies hot water through its own tap.

The immersion heater which is the cheapest electric water-heater to buy. It consists simply of the heater unit that is fitted to an ordinary hot-water tank or cylinder, which must be lagged to prevent wastage of heat. This can be used to heat the water in summer and in winter it can be used in conjunction with a solid fuel boiler to heat the water and supply a limited amount of central heating if necessary.

All electric water-heaters have their own built-in thermostats to keep the water at a steady temperature and to turn off the current when the water is hot enough.

Are the oil-filled electric radiators absolutely safe? Does the oil smell?

The special type of oil is sealed inside the radiator so there can be absolutely no smell whatsoever from the oil. The radiator is completely safe because the element is never in contact with the oil and the temperature can be controlled by thermostat.

How do you know the size of electric fire to get for a particular room?

Providing you know the size of the room you will not be far out if you allow 1 watt for every cubic foot of space for full heating and a $\frac{1}{2}$ watt per cubic foot for background heating. It is important that the heater should be of sufficiently high loading to ensure satisfaction. It is false economy to buy a smaller fire or radiator than is actually required to heat the room.

I am told you can buy an inexpensive tubular electric heater which can be installed in an ordinary cupboard to turn it into an airing cupboard. Which is it?

Any short tubular electric heater can be used for this purpose; it is advisable to arrange grilles at the top and bottom of the door to maintain a proper circulation of air if the cupboard is to be used to dry wet clothes.

I want to buy a heater for the bedroom which we can put on at night and in the morning when we get up during the cold weather.

For occasional heating of this sort I recommend the reflector electric fires and the panel gas fires or free-standing gas fires that fit into the hearth.

We want to keep the temperature of our bedroom reasonably warm all through the winter. Can you suggest a form of heating that will take off the chill without making the room stuffy?

The pastel-coloured independent oil-filled electric radiators are excellent for this purpose. So are the electric and gas convector radiators; oil-burning radiators are also satisfactory. The electric tubular heaters provide another suitable alternative; they operate at black heat and so are particularly economical on fuel.

Is it safe to install an electric heater in the bathroom?

Yes, providing the fire is mounted high up on the wall and is switched *outside* the bathroom so that the user must go outside the bathroom to switch on and off. All water pipes in the bathroom should be earthed as an extra precaution.

Please suggest a suitable form of heating for a bathroom, not electric!

An oil-burning radiator complete with towel rail is ideal. The Morris and Hurseal models are specially adapted for this purpose.

Can you suggest a cheap method of heating a small hall in winter?

The tubular electric heaters are inexpensive to buy and running costs are low because they operate at black heat. This is a suitable method of heating a small hall. Alternatively, you could have an oil-burning radiator which costs much more to buy—

from about £17, but they operate on about 1 gallon of paraffin for about 40 hours. Other alternatives are an electric oil-filled radiator, either fixed or portable or free standing, *or* an electric convector heater *or* a gas-operated convector heater. Why not go along to your local dealer or gas and electric showrooms, and to your ironmonger, and have a look at these units?

What are the advantages of an electric convector heater?

These heaters combine extra safety with efficiency because the heating unit is entirely enclosed in the casing, and the room is heated evenly by the drawing in of the cold air at the bottom of the heater, which is warmed as it passes over the heating unit, and is then circulated through grilles at the top. In one type of convector heater a fan is incorporated to speed up the circulation of warmed air. Yet another type is a combined radiant and convector heater; the convector unit is totally enclosed and independently controlled. Gas or oil-burning heaters are also made.

Is calor gas more expensive than ordinary town gas, and what can it be used for?

According to the makers, calor gas costs approximately twice as much as ordinary town gas but, of course, this is only very rough estimate because the price of town gas varies considerably. It can be used for heating domestic water, cooking, to operate gas fires, gas-operated refrigerators, gas wash-boilers, laundry irons and lighting installations. It is particularly useful in the country where there is neither electricity nor gas, and for caravans and holiday bungalows. It is important to ensure a regular supply.

Is there any advantage to be gained by choosing an appliance that has been approved by the Coal Utilisation Council?

Yes, definitely, because this is an independent body of experts who give honest test reports about products. Not all manufacturers submit their products so that it does not necessarily mean that because a unit does not come within the list of approved products it is unsatisfactory. But if you do choose a product from the CUC recommended list of products you may be sure you are buying a reliable product that will do all that the manufacturer's claim for it.

LIGHTING

What size of electric filament lamp should I buy for normal household use?

It is tremendously important to have sufficient light for a particular purpose—reading, writing, sewing, preparing food, repairing the car and so on. A 100-watt lamp is the size usually recommended for table lamps and ceiling fittings in small rooms. Floor standards usually need at least 150 watts, and this should also be the minimum total wattage of multi-lamp ceiling fittings but they can be made up by a number of 40- or 60-watt lamps if you wish. Wall brackets usually take 40- or 60-watt lamps in each holder, but if the shades are small and there is sufficient general lighting in the room, 25-watt lamps can be used. Most good shades are made for a definite size of lamp and it is advisable to use the size recommended because if the shades are too small they are (with the exception of glass and metal) likely to scorch.

What sort of lighting should I have in my kitchen?

Fluorescent lighting is excellent for the kitchen because it can be arranged to avoid all shadows, but you need to experiment with it to discover the ideal positions. Watch especially for shadows cast by the lamps when you are working near the walls. Hanging cupboards over work surfaces can be fitted with short architectural lamps to light the work surfaces. Similar short lamps can be fitted inside dark cupboards.

I have been told I ought to ask for the coiled-coil type of electric filament lamps in preference to the single coil type. Do you think the coiled-coil type are worth the extra money?

The difference in price is very small and the coiled-coil type of lamp gives up to 20 per cent. more light for the same current consumption as a single coil lamp, so it is well worth the slight extra cost.

What is the difference between pearl, silica and clear electric lamps? Which do you recommend for general use in the home?

The pearl lamps, which give no less light than the clear lamps, are recommended for general use in the home. If you want a very soft diffused light buy a silica internally-coated lamp. Always avoid clear lamps for domestic purposes except where you deliberately wish to throw hard shadows. And choose coiled-coil in preference to single-coil filament lamps.

How should a dressing table be lit?

One good method is to have a light on each side with a half-shade that can be turned to give a strong direct light on your face. Or to have 12-inch architectural lamps on both sides of the mirror.

Can you recommend the necessary lighting for a normal sized bathroom?

General and mirror lighting are necessary. Choose between a totally enclosed ceiling fitting for a filament lamp of 100 watts, and a 12-inch architectural lamp above the mirror, or on each side of the mirror, *or* a pair of short 12- or 20-watt fluorescent lamps, and the architectural lamps to light the mirror.

Can you buy contemporary-styled gas lighting fittings?

Yes, certainly. Your local Gas Showrooms will be able to show you some examples of attractive contemporary fittings.

Are there any bright incandescent oil lamps that make no noise?

Definitely, yes. If you need a more powerful light than these give you can buy one of the big pressure burners which are most efficient and make only a little noise when operating. The Tilley Lamp Co. is one of the firms that specialises in these lamps.

What is the best position for a bedside reading lamp?

Each bed should have a separate switched reading lamp placed, if possible, off-centre and fairly high to prevent your sitting in your own light and knocking it when making the bed. Fit at least 60-watt lamps for this purpose.

NURSERY

We are building a new night nursery and are undecided how to heat it. Can you help?

Apart from the heating method being completely safe in itself the unit must stand firmly and be fairly heavy so that it cannot be knocked over. The electric oil-filled radiators are ideal for the nursery because they are so safe; electric convector heaters are good, too, and you may like to have a look at the gas convector heaters. Electric tubular heaters could also be used, or continuous burning solid fuel fires or stoves.

What form of heating do you recommend for a day nursery?

A continuous burning solid fuel fire, properly guarded, cannot be improved although the solid fuel stoves, with openable fronts, are perhaps less trouble since they do not need to be guarded in the same way. If you do not wish to install solid fuel units, choose between an electric oil-filled radiator, an electric or gas convector or, if the room is quite small, tubular electric heaters.

Please suggest a suitable flooring for a nursery?

You want to choose a flooring with a warm finish; I suggest linoleum, plastic or compressed cork. All are easily cleaned. Choose washable rugs to give extra cosiness to the room.

Which do you consider the ideal aspect for a nursery?

I would choose south-east because this is bright and sunny in the morning and cool in the afternoon and evening.

I want to arrange a section of the nursery wall as a blackboard. What is the easiest way to do this?

Either buy a blackboard and fix it to the wall or paint the area with special blackboard paint. Alternatively, you might like

to consider a wall panel of laminated plastic which can be easily washed down when the child has finished drawing on it.

Our second child is much too old to be sleeping with us and we would like him to sleep with his young brother in the nursery. Unfortunately there isn't space for his bed in the nursery and we haven't a spare bedroom.

Have you thought of investing in two-tier bunk beds which are now being sold at many of the large stores ? The two beds would fit comfortably into the space now occupied by your elder child's bed and he would love the idea of sleeping "aloft"!

The walls of the new nursery look very bare; we cannot afford to buy pictures and we are not clever enough to paint pictures on the walls ourselves. Have you any ideas?

I have seen some quite attractive transfer pictures designed specially for the nursery walls. You can buy these at many stationers. Place them about half-way down the wall so that the child can look at them without craning his neck.

Baby is still too young to manage without a high chair which makes it difficult when we go away for week-ends by car. Is it possible to buy an inexpensive folding high chair?

Yes! There is a folding high chair made of tubular steel which clips on to the back of almost any dining chair *or* car seat. The back rest and seat are made of heavy plastic leather which is easy to wipe down, and the tubular steel is heavily stove-enamelled. It weighs $4\frac{1}{2}$ lb. and folds flat for easy storage; manufacturers are Derek Products Ltd.

My small daughter is a restless sleeper and her bed is narrow. I want to find a way of securing the bedclothes to give her enough freedom to turn round but a firm tuck-in to prevent her falling out of bed.

Arrange a box pleat down the centre of the bed from the foot upwards. Do this both with the top sheet and the blankets and tuck them in very firmly at the sides. Your daughter will then have room to move about but will be unlikely to untuck the bedclothes at the sides.

PAINTING AND DECORATING

How do you assess the quantity of paint, etc., required for interior decoration?

		Surface in sq. ft. covered by 1 gallon of paint.	
Type of Paint.	Type of Surface.	One Coat	Two Coats
Oil paint (glossy)	Prepared Wood	600	330
,, ,, ,,	Plaster	450	250
Oil paint (flat)	Prepared Wood	500	275
,, ,, ,,	Plaster	400	230
Water paint	Smooth	310	

I want to apply a flat paint to a kitchen wall that was formerly decorated with oil-bound distemper, and now has an emulsion paint on it. The walls, which are subjected to quite a lot of steam, are inclined to flake and I am wondering how I should prepare them.

It is essential to remove both existing coats before applying the flat paint, and you can do this with "Quickstryp" Emulsion Paint Remover, and the walls will be ready for painting without any further preparation.

Can a washable wallpaper be used in the kitchen?

Yes, but it must be specially treated to resist steam; regard it as spongeable and not washable. Seek the advice of your wallpaper retailer before buying. It is inadvisable to have wallpaper in a kitchen where there is bad condensation or in the part of the kitchen where the steam is greatest.

Please suggest suitable finishes for the walls of our new bathroom.

Tiled walls are extremely suitable for a bathroom and they can be bought in an attractive range of colours; they could be used to dado height and the remainder of the wall finished with an enamel or high-gloss paint, which could be used also for the ceiling. If you wish to economise you could fit plastic tiles. Glazed asbestos sheeting gives an even cheaper finish and it can be fitted over plaster. If you do not wish for any of these materials why not consider painting the walls and ceiling with a good quality enamel or glossy paint? Arrange splash-backs of plastic or tiles round the bath and behind the hand-basin.

I believe a different technique has to be employed when you apply enamel as against paint.

The only difference is that you flood on the enamel and the last brushing should be very, very light to avoid brush marks.

I have read about a synthetic quick-drying lacquer which gives a highly glossy finish and withstands heat up to boiling point. Can you give me the name of it?

I think you are referring to "Valspar", and I can thoroughly recommend this product for the purposes for which it is sold.

I admire the way some amateur painters are able to get a smooth surface to their work. How is this achieved?

By flooding on the paint from a heavily loaded brush, then wiping the brush dry on the edge of the paint tin, and removing the surplus paint with the brush. "Tears" form when too much paint is left on the surface.

We had trouble with the damp course of our house which has now been put right. But the ugly dark patches remain on the outside living room wall. Do they have to be specially treated before redecorating?

It would be wise to apply two coats of aluminium or "knotting" paint before applying any other finish to the wall.

I want to paper the walls of my dinette which forms part of the kitchen but I am afraid the steam will affect the paper. Is there a special type of paper I should buy?

Choose a wallpaper that can be sized and varnished—your wallpaper retailer will advise you. So long as the kitchen is properly ventilated and not unduly exposed so that the walls are cold, and therefore liable to heavy condensation, it should be safe to use ordinary wallpaper, or a spongeable paper. But avoid wallpaper in the part of the kitchen where steam is worst.

We have a large family of young children and are wondering if we should be silly to have our walls papered; we are getting rather tired of washable distemper though we realise its merits where there is a young family!

Washable distemper or emulsion paint is usually the better proposition where there are young children because it is so easy to sponge down. But the situation has been changed overnight by a solution called "Fend" which can be painted over the wallpaper (or distemper!) to leave an invisible film which enables all sorts of marks to be rubbed off without their penetrating to the paper. It is so new that it is impossible to say how long the treatment will last but early tests have been most encouraging, and I think it is worthy of your consideration.

What is the correct procedure when you paint a room?

1. Prepare the ceiling and walls. 2. Prepare the woodwork. 3. Paint the ceiling. 4. Paint the walls. 5. Paint the door. 6. Paint the window frames. 7. Paint the picture rail. 8. Paint the skirting. 9. Paint or stain the floor.

Does it matter whereabouts you start painting a door?

Yes, because you should avoid painting over parts already done or you will spoil the smoothness of the finish. Begin by painting the moulds (1) and panels (2), then the two middle vertical "stiles" (3) between the panels, then the horizontal or cross strips (4) and finally, the two outer side "stiles" and the door edges (5).

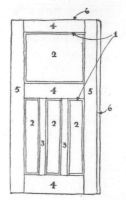

G

Our living room has a very low ceiling. What colour would you suggest for decorations?

You can increase the apparent height of the room by decorating the ceiling and walls in the same colour; the absence of a picture rail is another asset if you want to give an impression of greater height. Choose a light colour.

Do you advise paint or distemper for a kitchen ceiling?

Paint or enamel is much more suitable for a kitchen ceiling than either distemper or whitewash because it is so easy to wash down, and it lasts much longer.

Does it matter if I apply a flat paint over an emulsion paint that has started to flake?

It certainly does because your flat paint will be likely to flake off too unless placed over a perfectly smooth surface. You can remove the emulsion paint most successfully with "Quickstryp" Emulsion Paint Remover which leaves the walls ready for decorating.

Do you advise wallpaper or emulsion or gloss paint for uneven plaster walls?

Wallpaper with rough texture will hide the uneven plaster better than paint. But wallpaper is not generally recommended for a kitchen or bathroom where there is a lot of steam; for these rooms I would advise lining the walls with paper before painting with a flat or gloss paint.

HOUSE MAINTENANCE AND REPAIRS

A small portion of my living room ceiling beneath a spare bedroom has become discoloured while the other half, beneath our own bedroom, remains quite unaffected. What is the reason for this?

Ceilings which suffer from condensation are the most likely to discolour and the ceilings with the unheated rooms above are the most likely to be affected by condensation. I imagine you will have more heating in your own bedroom than in your spare room and this is why the ceiling beneath the spare room has discoloured while the remainder, beneath your own room, is unaffected. If you do not wish to increase the heating in the spare bedroom you could place an insulating material (Vermiculite, glass fibre quilt or aluminium foil) over the part of the living room ceiling that has discoloured. It will be necessary to have the ceiling redecorated because there is nothing you can do to restore the colour of the existing decorating.

Is there a cure for efflorescence striking through from the brickwork and breaking down paint and lifting wall-paper?

This type of efflorescence often occurs in a new house when paint or distemper is applied too quickly before the building has had time to dry. I cannot recommend any chemical treatment to neutralise or destroy efflorescence; any treatment applied to the surface to suppress evaporation is likely to be harmful. But you can apply an emulsion or water paint which allows the efflorescence to work through and if you brush it off frequently it should eventually all work out of the walls.

What is the best way to stop draughts blowing through inside doors?

Big gaps round doors need adjusting by a joiner—they have most likely warped or are due to bad workmanship when they were first hung. Normally, however, you can help considerably by fitting rubber piping or a flexible metal strip round the top and down the side of the doors. Rubber mouldings and draught excluders that lift up and down with the action of the door are recommended for the bottom of the doors.

Please advise on a cheap solution for draughts blowing up between the floorboards of an old house.

Linoleum is one of the cheapest ways of stopping draughts blowing through the floorboards. It should be fitted to reach from skirting to skirting all over the room. Close carpeting is another good way to prevent draughts coming up between the floorboards.

If you do not want to cover the boards in either of these ways, you can use a mastic sealing compound to fill the gaps; when this is dry it can be stained to match the floor. Thin fillets of wood can also be used in this way. Yet another method is to cover the floor with sheets of $\frac{3}{16}$-inch, $\frac{3}{8}$-inch or $\frac{1}{2}$-inch insulating fibre building board costing only a few coppers a square foot; it is used as an underlay for carpet or linoleum and is particularly useful if you have a carpet that has gone thin with wear. Rubber-backed needle-loom carpeting is particularly good for keeping out the draughts but it is inadvisable to use this where there is a lot of traffic such as in a living room.

The skirtings in our house have shrunk away from the floorboards leaving large gaps. What can I do to prevent the draughts blowing through?

Nail quarter-round strips of wood to the floor close to the skirting then paint them to match the skirting.

The windows of our temporary home fit badly and let in a lot of cold air. Is there anything that I, a mere house-wife, can do about it?

The windows really need the attention of a joiner but you can help keep out the draughts by putting up heavy curtains reaching to the floor. However, it would be very much cheaper to get a joiner to put the windows right for you!

We have just moved into a new house and find that the doors of the house and doors and drawers of all our furniture are sticking; they were all right when we moved in and the furniture is of good quality.

It is possible that your house was still damp when you moved in; new houses take several months to dry out completely, and a few weeks of damp will affect any furniture. It should recover as the house dries out; sprinkle the drawer runners in the framework with a very little French chalk to help them to run more smoothly. The doors of the house should improve as they dry out.

How should one tackle the problem of streaming walls due to condensation in a kitchen?

Improved ventilation helps considerably and an electric extractor fan fitted to a hole in the wall or in a window pane will draw out most of the steam. A sheet metal hood placed over the cooker and sink, with a fan at the top, is another way of getting rid of steam but the appearance is less elegant. Use a plastic emulsion paint if you wish but see that the surface is thoroughly cleaned down and no gloss remains before applying the emulsion or the moisture may get behind the paint and cause blisters. Personally, I prefer a hard matt paint and the discomfort of mopping up pools, which should be almost non-existent if you have an extractor fan.

The country cottage we have just taken has not got a damp course and there are signs of damp. Is there a satisfactory alternative?

If it is impractical to construct a new damp course you can resort to one of the following: metal foil applied to the inside surface of the plastered walls which is kept in position with a waterproof adhesive; a 1-inch layer of cement and sand to which a waterproofing material is added, and applied to the inside brickwork from floor to ceiling after the plaster has been

REFRIGERATORS AND STORAGE
OF PERISHABLE FOODS.

How much does it cost to run a 'frige?

This depends upon the size you choose. A 5-cu. ft. refrigerator of the compression type consumes just over 1 unit of electricity in 24 hours, and at the average price of electricity that would work out at about 1d. However, an absorption refrigerator of the same size would use between two and three times as much electricity. In addition to the cost of running you need to consider cost of maintenance and convenience. Advantages claimed for the absorption are that it is completely silent and has no moving parts and therefore nothing to wear out. For the compression, the makers claim it freezes much more quickly, and is cheaper to run: there are more compression units than absorption units from which to choose.

Supposing I want to buy a 'frige of 1½ cu. ft. capacity how much would I have to pay for hire purchase?

You could put between £6 10s. and £8 down and pay quarterly instalments of between £5 5s. and £6 7s. 6d. You could also hire one if you live in certain areas and occupy a house belonging to the Council for as little as 2s. 6d. per week.

How much do domestic refrigerators cost?

From about 38 gns. for the 1½ cu. ft. models up to about £150 for the 8 cu. ft. and 9 cu. ft. models. When and if purchase tax is lifted these prices will fall considerably.

How does one choose the size of refrigerator to buy?

As a rough guide you want to allow 1 cu. ft. of space inside the cabinet for each member of the household. This means that if there are three of you in family you need a 3 cu. ft. refrigerator. If, however, you have a young baby whose food will not take up much space in the 'frige for a year or two, which means there is only your husband and yourself, you can manage on a $1\frac{1}{2}$ to 2-cu. ft. model. You will then have to pack much more carefully and avoid bulky containers which take up more space than they really need.

Can you give me any tips about snags to look for when choosing a refrigerator?

Shelves with little ridges at the front that stop the dishes sliding out easily.

Too long and narrow milk-bottle compartments that make it difficult to reach the bottle at the back.

Shelves without adequate supports both at the sides and at the back often have a nasty habit of slipping out of position and down crash your precious dishes of food!

Watch too, for a badly-fitting door which prevents a good refrigerating temperature inside the cabinet and sends up your fuel bills.

As a good general tip: buy a refrigerator made by a well-known manufacturer and then you will be sure of buying one of the best available because these established manufacturers have spent many years perfecting their 'friges and you are sure of a good after-sales service.

Do refrigerators interfere with TV and radio reception?

No. The refrigerators working on AC mains do not interfere with either TV or radio reception and those operating on DC mains have suppressors fitted.

Does it save electricity (or gas) to turn off the refrigerator at nights?

No, apart from having a detrimental effect on the food (which needs to be kept at a consistently low temperature) this habit does not save any fuel because the coldness of the cabinet has to be built up again during the day and more fuel is consumed this way than if the 'frige is able to operate normally all the time.

I live in the country without either electricity or gas; is it possible for me to have a refrigerator?

Yes! You can operate an absorption model by oil or butane gas.

What is the ideal temperature for storing food—can it be attained in the ordinary larder?

Food keeps good when the temperature is low enough to stop the bacteria present in all perishable foods from functioning—below 50 deg. F. Preferably between 42 and 45 deg. F. Only in very cold weather is this temperature attainable in the average larder; older houses with basement larders were able to maintain this temperature for a longer period of the year.

Is it possible to have a refrigerator built into my new kitchen cupboard fitments?

This can nearly always be arranged; the 1½ cu. ft. models are often made to be fitted in this way, and the larger refrigerators can be adapted; consult your dealer about this and I feel sure he will be able to help.

If you had the choice between a table-top refrigerator and one with a rounded top, which would you choose?

I would choose the table-top every time because of the extra working space it affords, but if you want to buy a larger refrigerator over about 4½ cu. ft. you may have to choose one with a rounded top. Models of from 1½ to 4½ cu. ft. capacities can be bought with table-tops.

Can I get a refrigerator to match my kitchen colour scheme or must it be in that clinical white?

Frigidaire are among the big firms making coloured refrigerators and they look most attractive.

Is there any reason why I shouldn't put the 'frige in the larder? We have just enough space for it.

Yes! There's a good reason why larders and other confined places are unsuitable for a refrigerator. The principle of refrigeration is that the heat, contained by all food, even a bottle of cold milk, must be removed if it is to be kept good. The warmth has to be circulated in the surrounding air, and that is why all refrigerators have grilles at the back. Unless this warm air can circulate freely the refrigerator will not work properly, and the larder will be much too warm and stuffy.

What is the ideal position for a refrigerator in the kitchen?

In the coolest part of the kitchen, close to the food preparation table and in a good light so that you can see what you are doing inside the 'frige—not all models have lights inside but it is a great help when they have. Avoid placing a refrigerator next to the cooker or boiler whenever possible; although the refrigerator is excellently insulated warm air flows in whenever the door is open and so the freezing unit has to work all the harder to keep the cabinet cool.

My new refrigerator temperature control is marked in numbers; I am at a loss to know which is highest and which is lowest temperature.

Setting No. 1 is the lowest and gives the highest temperature in the cabinet. When you want to make ice you turn the thermostat to the lowest temperature, i.e. the highest number on the dial, or MAX. The temperature range inside the cabinet usually ranges from about 48 deg. F. to 28 deg. F. in steps of 2 deg.; most manufacturers issue instructions with their refrigerators and it is advisable to follow these carefully.

Which is the coldest part of the 'frige? I've noticed the temperature is not the same all over the cabinet.

The coldest part of the 'frige is directly under the freezer and the least cold is in the opposite top half of the 'frige next to the freezing unit. The cold air from the freezer falls, is warmed as it passes the food and then rises again to be cooled once more by the freezing unit before circulation.

What about the placing of food in a refrigerator. Does it matter where it is put?

It matters very much! Fish should be put in the coldest part of the 'frige directly under the freezer; it can be placed in the drip tray if you like, on an upturned saucer or rack to prevent it lying in its own juices. See it is well covered to prevent the odour spreading and being absorbed by other foods. Meat goes on the next shelf down below the fish; cooked meat and milk puddings, blancmanges, etc., can go on the bottom shelf. Butter, margarine, cheese and milk go on the middle shelf next to the freezer. Any savoury dishes with strong flavourings such as onions or lemons, should go next to the freezer at the top so that the circulation of air takes the odour right back to the freezer where the odour is lost and does not circulate to other food in the cabinet.

Should all food be wrapped in a refrigerator?

Yes! The only exceptions are eggs which need to breathe to keep fresh, trifles and jellies, etc., which are not left in the 'frige very long and a cover would often spoil their appearance. Grease-proof paper is very useful for wrapping dry foods especially cooked and uncooked meats and fish. The plastic bags are also excellent and the plastic and glass-covered refrigerator dishes are also good. All give protection against the natural tendency of food to "dry out" a little in the 'frige because of the very dry air, and they prevent the odour of one food being carried to another. Dairy produce is particularly susceptible to tainting from strong smelling foods. Fresh meat can, if necessary, be left uncovered.

The ice cube drawers in my refrigerator always seem to be frozen to the shelf of the freezer when I go to take them out. Why is this?

I think you may fill the drawers too full of water. They should

never be more than three-quarters filled with water or it overflows before freezing and causes a general freeze-up all round the drawers. Dry the outsides of the drawers too, to prevent them sticking because of their being wet when placed in the freezer.

What is an easy way to remove ice cubes when they come from the freezer?

Hold them under a running cold water tap for a few moments.

How are the coloured ice cubes made?

Most often with sweetened fruit juice or a little harmless colouring which is mixed with the water before freezing.

Is it safe to store food in a refrigerator when it is not working?

Never! The airy pantry is a much better place for food in these circumstances.

Is it right to store tinned food and jams, etc., in the 'frige?

No! Because these foods are already preserved! It is therefore a waste of valuable space to store them in a refrigerator but you can, of course, chill canned foods such as fruit juice, meat, etc., that you want to serve cold.

Is there any reason why I shouldn't put a jelly straight into the refrigerator when it has been made and is still warm?

Yes, indeed! It not only sends up the temperature in the refrigerator and may send some of the food bad, but it also makes the freezer work overtime trying to cool the cabinet down, and it causes additional icing on the freezer which impedes efficient operation. ALWAYS see that food is quite COLD before putting it into the refrigerator!

I am told that if I pack my refrigerator carelessly I interfere with its efficient operation. Is this right?

Yes! The efficiency of a refrigerator depends largely upon a continual circulation of air which results from the cold air from the freezing unit falling, becoming warmed as it passed through the food and rising again; when food is carelessly packed this essential circulation of air is often impeded.

How often should a 'frige be defrosted?

At least once every 10 or 14 days. Personally I defrost my refrigerator every week because I clean it each week and like to defrost it at the same time, but this is not strictly essential.

How can you be sure you get the refrigerator perfectly sweet and clean when you defrost it?

Defrost by setting the control knob at the highest (warmest) temperature and remove all food. Remove also the ice drawers and empty them, then dry. Leave the cabinet door open till all the frost has melted. Wash out the cabinet with a weak solution of bicarbonate of soda, rinse well with cold water and dry thoroughly. See that the drip tray or bowl is placed under the freezer to catch the drips during defrosting. When defrosting and cleaning has been completed turn the control knob to normal and put back the food.

Must all food be removed before defrosting?

Yes, because the temperature is allowed to rise to allow the ice to melt and this is bad for the food. In addition the ice may drip onto the food and spoil it. In one or two models defrosting is automatic and then food need not be removed.

I find my butter is much too hard for spreading when it leaves the refrigerator. Have you any suggestions?

Take the butter you need for the next meal out of the refrigerator a few hours before you want to use it and leave at room temperature then it will be just right for spreading. Two of the newest refrigerators incorporate "Buttadors" which consist of a compartment in the door of the refrigerator where the butter can be kept at spreading temperature by means of a very minute heater in the floor of the compartment. This is ideal so long as you follow the manufactuer's advice and do not leave butter in for longer than a day or two; if left for a long time in the compartment it may turn rancid because of the warm temperature. It is controlled by thermostat.

Is it possible to make food fresh again once it has gone off by putting it into the refrigerator?

Never! Food that has gone off should be thrown away at once because it can cause food poisoning and serious illness. A refrigerator's job is to keep food from going off and not to revive it once this has happened.

Is it true that raw pastry can be stored in the 'frige for use during the week?

Yes! It improves by being kept cold, and should be wrapped

in greaseproof paper, and portions cut off as you want to cook it.

Should salad ingredients be washed before storing?

Yes! Shake out most of the water before storing them either in a plastic bag or special container in the refrigerator, or in a bowl or saucepan with a lid on it.

Can food taken from the refrigerator and left in a hot room during a meal be put back again into the refrigerator without harming?

Yes! It is better to prevent the food deteriorating for most of the time than not at all.

I have a full-width freezing compartment right across the top of my refrigerator and I am wondering if I can freeze my own food in this compartment?

No! There is a good deal of confusion on this point. The purpose of these full width freezers is to enable the housewife to store a large quantity of frozen food in her refrigerator for some days. The temperature is lower than in the cabinet, being usually between 12 to 20 deg. F. In order to freeze food you must have a temperature of zero or below and there are one or two units coming on to the market consisting of a freezing compartment operating at this necessary low temperature, with a separate door, together with a compartment operating at normal food storage temperatures to keep foods from day to day in the usual way. Or you can buy a big freezing unit operating at zero temperature if you have a lot of food to freeze. You can store the food in this unit till you want to use it.

How long can the quick-frozen foods be stored at home?

Providing they are brought home quickly from the freezer at

the shop and are perfectly hard and firm when they arrive, they will keep from 2 to 3 days in the ice-making compartment of the refrigerator. Or if you have a full-width freezing compartment across the top of your refrigerator you can keep these foods for 1–2 weeks according to type. Without a refrigerator, you can wrap them in several thicknesses of newspaper and place them in the coolest part of your larder for not more than 24 hours.

Can frozen food be recooked within a day?

On no account should it be recooked after thawing and the initial cooking; it can be most dangerous.

How can food be kept fresh without a refrigerator?

Meat keeps best when it is hung or placed on a rack lightly covered to keep away flies and dust. On no account exclude the air or it will go bad quickly.

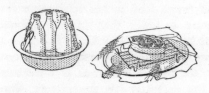

Fish keeps in a dish raised on a saucer or small rack to prevent it resting in its own juices; it should be covered with muslin or clean cloth to keep off flies and dust. It should not be kept for more than a few hours except when very fresh and in cold weather. Usually it is better to cook the fish when you bring it home and store it dry, covered with muslin.

Milk is best left in the bottles in which it is delivered. In hot weather the bottles can be stood in a dish containing water, and covered with a piece of thick cloth (such as Turkish towelling) with the ends in the water, and the dish placed in a draught. Jugs and basins containing custard or cream must be covered, preferably with muslin or something equally light and they can be stored in a similar way.

Fats and oils should be kept in the dark because the light helps to destroy vitamins and hastens rancidity.

Cheeses can be stored in a plastic food bag with the end open to allow it to "breathe". Greaseproof paper will also keep it fresh so long as the ends are left open. But when bought by the pound, cheese should not be stored more than a few days.

Eggs should be kept in a cool, airy place, preferably in an egg rack so that the air can circulate round them.

Fruit and vegetables store best in a vegetable rack with slatted wooden shelves or tubular wire baskets; but they must not be stored longer than necessary because they lose their nourishment quickly when stored. Salad ingredients keep in a large bowl covered with a plate to exclude light and air.

COOKERY

Whereabouts should food be placed in the oven?

This depends entirely upon the food you are cooking. The hottest part of the oven is at the top, and the bottom part is the coolest. Small pastries, small cakes and other dishes requiring quick cooking should be placed near the top of the oven. Large cakes, joints of meat and dishes requiring rather longer cooking time at a more moderate heat should be placed in the middle of the oven. Food needing long slow cooking, like milk puddings and casseroles, should be placed near the bottom of the oven.

N.B.—The position of the heating elements in some electric cookers varies and manufacturers' instructions must be followed.

Is it necessary to heat up the oven before putting in all types of food or does this only apply to cakes and meat, etc.?

Some modern cooks claim it is possible and desirable to cook most foods by placing them in a cold oven but I still believe the best results are obtained by pre-heating the oven to the necessary temperature before the food is put in.

COOKERY TERMS.

How much is a "gill"? The exact amount appears to vary in different parts of the country.

You are right, and it is most confusing. Strictly 1 gill means $\frac{1}{4}$ pint. Many cookery books avoid using this term by describing the amount as a fraction of a pint which is much clearer.

What does the cookery book mean when it talks about "blanching" food?

White meats and vegetables are blanched to preserve the colour; almonds and chestnuts are blanched to enable the skins to be removed easily. Put the food in cold water and bring to the boil. Drain and plunge straight into cold water.

What is "seasoned flour"?

Flour to which a sprinkling each of salt and pepper has been added. Proportions are $1\frac{1}{2}$ tablespoonfuls of flour to $\frac{1}{2}$ teaspoonful salt and $\frac{1}{4}$ teaspoonful pepper.

What is a bouquet garni?

A bunch of herbs. A sprig each of marjoram, thyme and parsley and sometimes a bayleaf are bound together, or tied in muslin, and cooked with liquid and other ingredients to give a savoury flavour. When enough flavour has been extracted the bouquet garni is lifted out of the cooking utensil.

How do you bake a pastry case "blind"?

Cut circles of greaseproof paper slightly larger than the pastry case, grease and place, greased side down, in the cases. Fill with dry beans, etc., and remove the filling 5 to 10 minutes before taking the pastry out of the oven.

What exactly is a "dropping consistency"?

This describes a texture for a cake or pudding mixture before cooking. Mixture held in a spoon over a mixing bowl should fall off within 4 or 5 seconds after the spoon is tilted.

How much is "a pinch" so often mentioned in recipes?

This is generally accepted to mean as much as can be held between the thumb and first two fingers.

FRYING, GRILLING and ROASTING

I am told it is wrong to prick meat during cooking because this lets out the juices and can make the meat flavourless. But how can you tell if the meat is done unless you test it?

Test it by all means, but not with a fork! Use the bowl of a spoon; if it resists pressure then the meat needs more cooking.

Can you suggest why the meat I grilled was tough and hard?

Did you grill a cheap cut which ought to have been done by a slow cooking method such as casseroling? Did you cook it too long? Was the heat too great? One of these points will give you the correct answer to your query!

I can never make croquettes without their breaking. What do I do wrong?

Is the frying fat hot enough to set the coating of the croquettes directly they are put in the pan? Do you apply the coating evenly? If you can answer "no" to one of these points you have found the reason why your croquettes break during cooking.

What makes rissoles and croquettes sodden and greasy?

This can be due to their being put into fat that is not hot enough to seal the coating and so the fat is absorbed by the food— the fat should be really hot before the food is put in. It can happen also through the coating being unevenly applied so that some patches of the food remain uncoated and absorb the fat. Yet another reason is due to putting too many croquettes into the fat at once and so lowering the temperature of the fat.

How can I prevent sausages from bursting when they are being cooked?

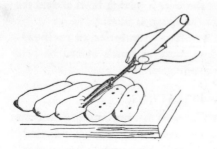

Prick them well before cooking. If the sausages are too tightly packed with meat the pricking alone does not always prevent them bursting and it is advisable to plunge them straight into boiling water before cooking.

What is the reason for fish and chipped potatoes being sodden and greasy?

They have been put into the fat to cook before the fat was hot enough to seal the food on the outside and prevent the fat from being absorbed. This trouble can also be caused to a lesser degree by failure to dry the chips that have been soaking in water, or fish that has been washed, before cooking. Avoid adding too much food to the fat at one time because this lowers the temperature of the fat and can make the food unpleasantly greasy.

The meat I cook is invariably hard and dry. I buy good cuts but this makes no difference.

Do you cook your meat in a very hot oven? Many people consider it necessary to seal the surface of the meat in a hot oven but the temperature should be lowered afterwards so that the meat cooks slowly and evenly right through. Try cooking it in a slower oven, and in a self-basting tin with a lid rather than in an open baking tin.

What is the reason for fat-sodden roast meat?

This often happens when the meat is stood directly in the baking tin without a meat rack beneath it, and it is resting in the liquid fat all the time it is cooking; this is apt to make it rather sodden. The answer lies in the use of a meat rack.

How should a joint be carved?

Invariably across the grain of the meat because this way it eats more tenderly. Usually beef is sliced very thinly, especially when eaten cold, while mutton and lamb are sliced fairly thickly. Medium thickness is recommended for pork and veal. Ham, tongue, brawn, etc., is sliced thinly.

I bought some prime steak to fry but when it eventually reached the table it was burned on the outside and underdone inside.

This was because your frying fat was too hot; next time cook at a lower temperature to allow the heat to penetrate right inside the steak. If the meat is very thick slice it before cooking.

What makes fried food greasy?

First, the fat was not hot enough when the food was put in to cook—a faint blue smoke should be rising from it. Second, the food was not drained properly before serving.

VEGETABLES

Why do potatoes break up in the water when they are being cooked?

Because the water has been boiling too quickly *or* because they are being cooked for too long a time.

I wish I knew why my lettuce always looks bruised and the edges of the leaves turn brown when I make salads.

Do you use a knife to cut the lettuce? This is usually the reason for these faults, especially when a kitchen knife is used. Instead, pull the leaves apart with the fingers—it looks better this way and the lettuce is much crisper.

Should a cucumber be peeled before serving?

This is entirely a matter of choice. It is correct to serve cucumber with or without the skin, although it is more digestible when the skin is removed. For decoration, a fork can be drawn down the cucumber before slicing to give a variegated effect.

Do you recommend that a pinch of bicarbonate of soda should be added to preserve the colour of green vegetables?

No! This should not be necessary if the greens are fresh and cooked in as little water as possible till done—and not *overdone*!

CAKES.

Is there a way of avoiding a Swiss roll cracking?

SUGARED GREASEPROOF
DAMP CLOTH

See that the oven is hot enough—a Swiss roll will crack when cooked in too cool an oven. It should be turned out on to greaseproof paper sprinkled with castor sugar, laid over a damp cloth and rolled up using the greaseproof paper as a lever while you roll.

My efforts to make a true sponge cake (without fat) have all ended in failure; my cakes are sticky and heavy. Why is this?

I wonder if you beat the eggs and sugar over water that is just a little too hot? This is a very common reason for failure with this type of recipe.

Although I took great trouble to sift the icing sugar and followed a good recipe for Chocolate Icing, mine was all speckled.

Did you overheat the icing when making? It wants to be warmed just enough to blend it.

What is the secret of preventing a piece of candied peel placed on top of a cake from sinking in?

Place it on the top of the cake *after* the top has set quite firmly! Never put it on before putting the cake into the oven because it is bound to sink in.

The cherries invariably sink to the bottom when I make a cherry cake.

This is because cherries are particularly heavy and for this reason it is always better to cut cherries in halves or quarters before using them in a cake. Sprinkle lightly with flour before adding to the cake mixture. The same applies to dates and figs to be used in a cake because they, too, are heavy.

Why does a cake sink in the middle?

Very often because the oven is too hot and the mixture rises too quickly then collapses. *Or* it may be that too much raising agent is being used *or* that the oven door was slammed and the cold air rushed in, lowered the oven temperature and caused the cake to collapse before it had set.

A cake I made looked cooked on the outside but was sticky and heavy on the inside when cut.

It sounds as if your cake was baked at too high a temperature for too short a time. *Or* that you made the mixture too wet.

What is the best way to test if a cake is done?

Touch the top of the cake very lightly with the finger-tip.

If it is cooked it will give only very slightly and rise again at once, *or* insert a warm skewer gently into the middle of the cake and if it comes away clean you will know the cake is cooked.

What makes a cake crack on the top?

The surface of the cake sets and begins to cook before the centre gets hot so that when the mixture rises it expands and cracks the top. This occurs when the oven is too hot and also when the cake is placed too near the top of the oven, which is usually the hottest part.

Why does fruit in a cake sink to the bottom?

This often happens because the cake mixture has been made too moist to support the fruit when it becomes warm. Cut large fruit into small pieces and sprinkle it lightly with flour before adding to the other ingredients.

I never seem able to make a really light cake. What do I do wrong?

There are several possible reasons for your failure to make a light cake. Do you use sufficient raising agent—either self-raising flour or plain flour and baking powder? Do you follow a good recipe and beat the eggs well, because the well-beaten eggs help to make the cake light. Do you cream the sugar and fat sufficiently well? It should look white and smooth when you have finished.

Is your oven hot enough? Is the cake cooled slowly out of a draught? Check up on all these points and your next cake should be beautifully light!

My cakes burn on the bottom; what can I do to prevent this?

It sounds as if the tins you are using are too thin and that they are not properly lined and protected. Always buy thick, good quality cake tins, and line them, for big cakes, with greaseproof paper; in the case of rich cakes use several thicknesses of grease-proof paper, and cover the outside of the tin with brown paper.

How can biscuits be kept fresh?

By storing them in an airtight tin *alone*. Never store biscuits with cakes or any other type of food because the biscuits will absorb any moisture from the other food and this makes them soft.

PUDDINGS AND SWEETS.

What makes the bottom of steamed puddings wet and slimy?

This happenes when the pudding is not properly covered and water gets inside during cooking.

How can I avoid stewed fruit breaking up and going pulpy?

Cook slowly, merely simmering, and avoid over-cooking.

My custard puddings and milk puddings containing eggs run to water during cooking. Why is this?

Because you allow them to boil. Cook in a very slow oven, and place the pie-dish in another dish containing water to help prevent the pudding boiling. Dishes containing eggs must never be allowed to boil.

The milk puddings I make are always of the stodgy type. Why?

Probably because you use too much grain; it could also be due to over-cooking or too hot an oven. Check on these points next time you make a milk pudding.

My children love junket but I never can get mine to set. Why?

Do you use enough rennet or junket powder? Is the milk at bloodheat when you mix it in—neither hot nor cold? These are the two important points to watch when making a junket.

I would love to know the secret of making light pancakes.

Begin with a well beaten thin pancake mixture, cook it on a hot greased girdle or in a well-greased frying pan (the pan must not be running in fat but just sufficiently well greased to stop the pancake sticking) and pour in only just enough pancake mixture to cover the bottom of the pan or most of the girdle—it should be wafer thin, and the girdle or frying pan piping hot.

What goes wrong when a blancmange refuses to turn out of a mould?

There are two possible reasons. Either the mould was insufficiently rinsed with cold water before the blancmange mixture was put in *or* the blancmange was not made sufficiently stiff.

What makes a blancmange collapse when it is turned out?

This usually happens when the blancmange is made too thin *or* when it is turned out before it has had time to set.

Suet crust puddings are often heavy. Why?

Because they have been put into, or over, water that was not boiling; cooking started before the water boiled and the crust had no time to rise before cooking. *Or* it can be due to the baking powder not being properly sifted and distributed evenly with the other ingredients. *Or* to too much liquid being used.

What can be done to prevent a roly-poly sticking to the pudding cloth?

Put the pudding into greased greaseproof paper before wrapping in the scalded and floured pudding cloth.

How do you tell when a roly-poly in a cloth is cooked— you can't see or test it without undoing the wrapping!

The pudding cloth begins to wrinkle as soon as the pudding is cooked—watch for this!

Can you advise me how to prevent fruit sinking to the bottom when making a table jelly?

Fruit generally sinks to the bottom of the mould for one of two reasons; either the jelly is not sufficiently stiff to support the fruit (it should be partly set before the fruit is added) *or* the fruit is added in too large pieces. Avoid these faults and you should be successful next time.

PASTRY

My short-crust pastry is always hard. Your hints please!

Do you cut down on the amount of fat you use? Not less than a quarter fat to flour should be used.

Do you rub the fat into the flour sufficiently thoroughly?

Do you add too much liquid?

Watch all these points and your short-crust should not be hard again!

I never seem able to make nice dry crusts for my fruit pies—the crusts are always sodden?

Make two slits in the top of the pie and allow the steam to escape during cooking BUT do this *only* when the pastry has set; it is useless to make the slits before putting the pastry into the oven, they just close up! Pie funnels achieve the same purpose and at the same time, help to support the pie crust.

Do tell me why my pie crust sinks in the middle.

I wonder if you make slits in your pie crusts *before* cooking? This is a common reason for sunken pie crusts. *Or* it can be caused by insufficient fruit, or other filling, in the pie dish. *Or* to the oven being too cool. Check up on these points next time you make a pie crust.

Sometimes my pastry is quite hard on the outside but uncooked inside.

This happens when the oven is too hot so that the outside gets cooked before the heat can penetrate to the inside and cook that. A slower oven is the answer.

Why does pastry sometimes blister?

There are three possible reasons for this. Either insufficient fat was used *or* the fat was not rubbed in properly *or* the pastry was too wet.

I would like to know how to stop pie crusts from shrinking from the edges of the pie-dishes.

If you avoid stretching the pastry when handling it you will have no bother of shrinkage from the edges.

CANNED FOOD.

Should I remove canned food from the can immediately it is opened?

Except in the case of fruit, which changes flavour when left in the can, the general rule is that food may be left in the can after it is opened. But personally, I prefer to store the contents in a glass or earthenware container; I believe the food tastes better and there is no danger of cutting the fingers on the raw edges of the can this way.

How long will canned food keep fresh after the can has been opened?

As long as the same sort of food would keep fresh if prepared in your own kitchen, from fresh ingredients.

Is it all right to eat food from a can that is badly bulged?

This depends on the sort of bulges! If the can bulges outwards at either end it is a "blown" can and the contents must be thrown

away. The bulge indicates that either the food acids have attacked the tin-plate and so generated hydrogen gas or that bacteria growing in the food has formed a mixture of gases. It is extremely unwise to attempt to reclaim the contents by boiling; the food should not be eaten under any circumstances whatsoever. Bulges inwards are usually the result of knocks during transit and do not harm the contents unless rusty.

Can food be canned at home?

Yes, but great care is necessary to ensure that the food is sterilised for sufficient time to destroy the bacteria normally existing in the food. The Worcester Can sealer is a well-tried product and is issued with full instructions.

JAM MAKING.

The jam I made recently crystallised and is uneatable. Why is this and what can I do to make it right?

Jam crystallises when it is allowed to boil before the sugar is properly dissolved. Or you may have used too much sugar. When the jam crystallises while in store it is often caused by the storage place being too hot. I am sorry to say there is absolutely nothing you can do to rectify this trouble.

Mould is forming on the top of my home-made jam, which was made from a good recipe and tastes lovely.

Was the fruit damp and soft when you made the jam? Were the jars at all damp? Were the jam jars properly covered before storing? Is the storage cupboard damp and stuffy? Any of these things can cause mould to form on the top of jam. Providing you remove all the mould from the top of the jam and clean the jar round about, and providing the jam tastes perfectly sweet and fresh, you can eat it after removing all trace of mould.

What makes jam ferment?

A badly ventilated, warm and damp storage cupboard is often responsible for jam fermenting.

My jam is very sticky; what have I done wrong? Will it keep?

You may have overboiled it, but don't worry, it will keep well.

For the first time in many years my home-made jam is not keeping well. I always use the same recipe and follow the same method so I am mystified as to the cause.

Did you use sufficient sugar? When making jam it is easy to accidentally omit a packet of sugar and this can upset the balance of the recipe. Alternatively I am wondering if you cut down on boiling time? This is a common cause of jam not keeping.

The last lot of jam I made was a bad colour. How can I prevent this happening again?

By making the jam immediately after the fruit has been prepared and skimming often while it is being made.

FRUIT BOTTLING.

Why does the fruit sometimes rise to the top of the jar?

Either because the fruit has not been packed closely enough *or* because too much sugar has been used to make the syrup (this makes it thick) *or* because the temperature has been raised too quickly during sterilising.

What makes fruit taste bitter after it has been bottled?

This sometimes happens with stone fruit when the stones are left in. It is advisable to remove most of the stones before bottling fruit; a few of the stones may be split and the kernels put in with the fruit to give extra flavour.

The fruit I have just bottled is cracked and broken. What is the reason for this?

Usually it is due to the temperature being raised too quickly during sterilising. The secret is to raise the temperature very slowly then the fruit remains whole, and much more important, the sterilising is much more efficient.

I took great care to make the syrup for my bottled fruit according to a good recipe, but it has gone cloudy. Why?

There are two possible reasons for this. The fruit may have been crushed when you put it into the bottles *or* the temperature may have been raised too quickly during sterilisation which results in the fruit breaking down and the syrup becoming cloudy because of the particles of fruit floating in it.

My bottled fruit has gone mouldy. Can I save it? What has caused it to go like this?

I am sorry to have to tell you there is absolutely nothing you can do to render mouldy fruit safe to eat. It is extremely dangerous and must be thrown away at once. Most frequently fruit goes mouldy when bottled because the temperature is raised too quickly during sterilisation which means that the inside of the fruit does not become properly sterilised; the bacteria, present in all fruits, multiplies, and mould results. It is important to raise the heat *slowly*!

The lovely colour of my plums was lost after bottling. What went wrong?

Did you prepare them some time in advance? Fruit should be bottled immediately it is prepared otherwise it is liable to become discoloured.

MISCELLANEOUS.

Do you recommend self-raising flour?

This depends entirely how you intend to use it. Self-raising flour is handy for general use but is unsuitable for rich cakes, which require less raising agent than that contained in self-raising flour. And I personally, prefer plain flour for pastry, for sauces and gravies (which are not so liable to go lumpy when made with plain flour). With a very plain mixture better results can often be obtained if a little baking powder is used in addition to self-raising flour, though I personally, always use plain flour and baking powder for this sort of cake.

I never know what sort of coffee to ask for; should it be fine, medium or coarse ground for everyday use?

This depends upon how you make your coffee. For instance, a fairly coarse ground coffee is suitable for use in most percolators but a finely ground coffee is better if you use an earthenware jug. When in doubt ask the coffee salesman for his opinion.

What makes a white sauce go lumpy?

Insufficient blending of ingredients before liquid is added; liquid added too quickly; sauce insufficiently stirred while the liquid is being added. Take the pan away from the heat when adding the flour to the fat and the liquid to the roux. Use plain flour. Vigorous whisking can often rescue a lumpy sauce, or it can be put through a sieve.

How can you stop a dark green ring forming round the yolk of a hard-boiled egg?

Providing the egg is fresh and you don't over-cook it, you can stop this discoloration by plunging the hard-boiled egg into cold water immediately it is cooked.

Is there an easy way to measure syrup and other sticky ingredients?

Balance a basin on your scales and weight the sticky ingredients straight into the basin, allowing for the weight of the basin.

What makes mayonnaise curdle when it is being made?

This is usually due to the oil being added too quickly to the yolk of egg at the beginning—an oil dropper to fit into the bottle is the answer to this problem. It can also be caused by careless separation of the egg whites and yolks; even a small amount of egg white sometimes induces curdling. Or it can be due to stale eggs and poor quality oil. Vigorous whisking will often save a curdled mixture and if this fails, a new egg yolk stirred well till smooth in another bowl then the curdled mixture added drop by drop, will help considerably.

WINE

What is the best way to store a few bottles of wine in a small house without a cellar?

You can usually store wine under the stairs quite satisfactorily. Lay the bottles on their sides so that the wine is in contact with the cork to prevent the cork shrinking and air reaching the wine.

At what temperature should wine be served?

White wine should be served chilled but not ice cold. Red wine should be served at room temperature.

How long will a bottle of table wine keep good after opening?

You can keep wine for two or three days if you put the cork back securely. Sherry and port wine will keep well for a much longer time if securely corked.

Can you help me to find my way about a wine list? I always experience difficulty in deciding which wine to order with the different courses at dinner.

The choice of wine is very much a matter of personal taste but there are a number of wines which definitely compliment certain food and others which do not go well. As a rough guide, serve a dry or medium dry Sherry or dry Madeira with soup and hors d'oeuvre, a dry white wine, such a Hock, Moselle, White Burgundy or Graves, with shellfish, oysters, fish, cold chicken, salads; a red wine, usually a light one like a Claret, with white meats, and a heavier wine, like a Burgundy, with the stronger flavoured meats; a sweet white wine, such as a Sauternes, with sweets and ices; a Vintage Port or liqueurs with coffee. Champagne can be served at almost any time, but ideally, it is drunk some little time before lunch is taken.

Can you advise me on the best of recent vintage years for wines?

The best of the recent vintages for most table wines are 1934, 1937, 1943, 1945, 1947, 1949, while for Port the years 1935, 1942, 1948 can also be added.

How much do you have to pay for a good bottle of wine?

You can get a good French red wine or a Bordeaux from about 6s. 6d. and a Burgundy from about 8s. 6d.

Does the age of wine matter very much?

Yes, indeed. A white wine is good at 3 years and a red wine at 5 years. See that the wine you buy is no younger than this.

I

PERSONAL PROBLEMS.

My skin is particularly dry and sensitive and I find  **that when I am cooking anything requiring a hot oven my face gets scorched by the sudden blast of hot air when I open the oven door.**

Heat rises, so crouch down as low as you can on your heels and get as far away as possible before opening the door; avoid make-up when cooking and apply a really good face cream, preferably of the quickly absorbed, feeding type.

After cooking the week-end joint my hair literally smells of roast meat! What can I do to prevent this happening?

Try wearing a thin chiffon scarf tied neatly around your hair while cooking; you can spray this with a little toilet water before you begin cooking. If you do not want to wear a scarf round your head, give your hair a thorough brushing and combing when you have finished cooking and spray it lightly with either a toilet water or a non-too-overpowering perfume.

When I have been peeling onions I am never able to get rid of the smell from my hands.

It is a good idea to wear thin rubber or plastic gloves or mitts when preparing onions. But if you do not like working in these, you will find that if you hold your hands under the cold water tap for several seconds after you have finished preparing the onions, before washing the hands in the normal way, the smell will go more easily.

Is there any quick way to remove stains from the hands?

Nail varnish remover is grand for removing fruit, vegetable and nicotine stains. Rub in a little hand cream after to keep the fingers soft and smooth.

I get frightfully tired when working about the house and I am told it is because my deportment is bad.

All jobs can be a great deal more tiring than they need be if approached with stiffened muscles and incorrect posture. Ballroom dancing is an excellent exercise in poise and a few lessons from an expert teacher would soon enable you to learn the secret of carrying the weight of your body equally between your two feet so that it is poised over them and not slumped forwards or backwards on one foot only. Knees should be straight, neither stiff nor bent, and you will find by learning to carry your body equally between your two feet that you will develop a certain "springiness" in your walk which will help you to "lift up" your body to its full height. When you stoop or bend learn to swing into the movement rhythmically, always smoothly, never jerkily, and it will prove to be much less tiring. DO see you have comfortable shoes which support your arches and wear sensible unrestrictive clothing when moving about the house.

What is the secret of packing a suitcase so that you get a lot into a small space?

Begin by packing heavy things, like shoes. Arrange them as closely as possible in an even layer and fit small articles, preferably of a soft nature, into the spaces and corners to level off and avoid waste space. Your heavy coat and suit should come next; fold to fit the size of the case exactly so that there is no wasted space in the corners. Pack your lighter weight clothes next and, finally, the silks and nylons, all to fit the case exactly. Knick-Knacks of all types can be used to fill any small gaps.

There is an art in folding garments. Button or fasten and

place them face downwards on a table or bed. Roll the side seam inwards to get a straight side. Turn back the sleeves and lay them along the side pieces then fold to a convenient size for your case.

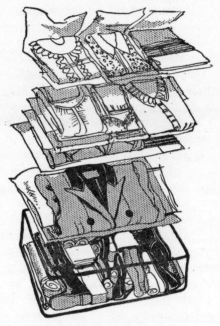

Inexpensive aids to easy, clean packing include the transparent shoe bags which prevent shoes marking your clothes, the light-weight plastic jars for make-up and the transparent envelopes to protect delicate fabrics and nylons.

CARE OF CLOTHES AND ACCESSORIES

Is it advisable that furs should be brushed?

Yes, use a fairly stiff brush to straighten out twisted and matted hairs, and to impart a gloss. A wide-toothed comb can also be used with good effect. This is particularly helpful in coats that are apt to get "sat out" at the back and for the collar that gets rubbed while being worn.

Is it advisable to clean a fur collar with one of the grease solvents?

Yes, it is quite a good way of getting rid of grease and traces of make-up but on no account allow the grease solvent to come in contact with the skin backing of the fur because it would harden this. I like the solvent called "Dabitoff" which has a pad on the top of the bottle that absorbs just the right amount of cleansing agent and avoids spills and too much coming out of the bottle at one time. "Thawpit" is another of this type.

Is there any method of reviving velvet?

It can be freshened by hanging up in a steamy atmosphere, as in a bathroom. Small areas can be steamed by holding in front of the spout of a boiling kettle and then drawing the material lightly across the upturned warm soleplate of an iron, wrong side

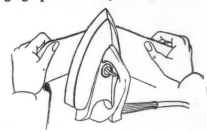

next to the iron. If the velvet needs thorough cleaning I advise you to send it for dry-cleaning.

Is there any means of reviving the texture of a not-so-new tweed suit?

Rub over lightly with a fine wire brush, a small section at a time, but be careful not to pull the threads as you work.

Can shine on dark suits be removed?

This depends how shiny the material is. It can certainly be reduced by sponging with ammonia and water—1 teaspoonful of ammonia to 1 pint of water. Hang in the open air to dry before pressing over a damp cloth.

Does a bathing suit need any special attention before being put away for the winter?

Wash it very thoroughly to remove all traces of salt water and make sure it is completely dry before storing in a cool, dry, dark place.

How can I revive the appearance of a rather old navy serge suit?

Sponge all over with a solution of ammonia and warm water—1 tablespoonful of ammonia to 1 pint warm water. Dry in the open air if possible.

I believe there is a way by which you can avoid leaving a ring round material that has been cleaned with a grease solvent.

Yes! Begin by placing the stained article over a pad of clean absorbent material and applying the solvent with a circular movement, beginning some distance from the mark and working inwards towards it, still with a circular movement. When the mark has been removed, place the garment to dry quickly.

I have just had a new dress cleaned and notice the shoulder pads have shrunk and gone hard.

A number of the new synthetic materials used to make shoulder pads do not dry clean satisfactorily and the cleaners advise that whenever possible shoulder pads should be removed before garments are sent for cleaning. In your case I advise you to remove the damaged shoulder pads in your dress and fit some new ones in their place.

Do dry cleaners generally undertake to remove stains from garments? A skirt I have just had cleaned came back with some stains still on it.

Providing the stains are removable and you ask especially for them to be removed, most cleaners will do their best for you. Always point out stains on a garment when you take it to be cleaned and the assistant will make a note of it to send to the works with the garment. Stains should be removed before cleaning because the hot air tumbling process through which the garments pass sets the stains further into the material. Unless special mention is made it is very easy for stains to go undetected by the cleaners and I imagine this is what has happened in your case. I advise you to take the skirt back and see whether your cleaners can help you to get the stains taken out.

Is there any way of ensuring that a woollen garment will not shrink and felt up when it is being dyed?

Unfortunately, no! Because of the nature of wool and the relatively high temperature needed to fix the dye, there must always be a risk of shrinkage and felting when woollen garments are dyed.

Is it necessary to remove buttons before sending clothes to be cleaned or dyed?

It is always better to remove them and it is a positive necessity in the case of fancy buttons which may not respond favourably to the cleansing agents. Also, there is always the danger that the buttons may come loose during the cleaning process and get lost.

What are the powder dry cleaners used at home for lightly soiled articles?

An absorbent powder, usually french chalk or powdered magnesia is used for cleaning lightly soiled woollen materials, furs, etc. Remove stains with a grease solvent and remove dust with a stiff brush, then spread out on a large piece of brown paper and cover with the powder, rubbing it gently in with the hands. Roll up and leave for a day or so before shaking and brushing out the powder.

What is the best way to clean buckskin shoes that are badly soiled?

Sponge with soap and water to clean then apply a white shoe cleaner sold specially for buckskin and follow the manufacturer's instructions about applying it.

How can make-up marks, chiefly powder, be removed from the collar of a dark suit?

Brush to remove any loose powder then rub with a circular movement using a soft cloth moistened with carbon tetrachloride. Or a little ammonia and water can be used—1 teaspoonful of ammonia to 1 pint of warm water.

Is it true that dry cleaning takes the body out of materials? If so, how can they be cleaned?

Dry cleaning should never take the body out of material; in my experience the more often clothes are cleaned the longer they last because dirt and grit that cling to the material wear it far more than the tumbling action to which the clothes are subjected in process of dry cleaning. Apart from this, it is essential from a hygienic point of view to have clothes cleaned regularly.

What is the correct method of cleaning pigskin?

Handbags, travelling bags, shoes, belts, etc., can be rubbed over with a cloth dipped in carbon tetrachloride, and occasionally rubbed up with a good furniture or shoe cream. Pigskin gloves can be washed.

Is it possible to buy the cleansing agents used by the cleaners and can these be used successfully at home?

White spirits and trichlorethylene are two of the most common cleansing agents used by the dry cleaners. White spirits is highly inflammable and must be used under specially guarded conditions, while the fumes from trichlorethylene can be highly injurious unless suitably controlled. Because of these dangers other quite efficient cleansing agents like carbon tetrachloride and benzene are sold for domestic use. A particularly good method of applying these cleansing agents is adopted by some firms I know who fix padded corks to the bottles through which the cleansing fluid filters slowly as you rub it over the fabric you want to clean.

Can clothes be moth-proofed? If so, who does the job?

Yes, clothes can be moth-proofed and this lasts for a year or two or until the clothes are cleaned or washed. Many of the big firms of dyers and cleaners will do the job for you.

Do you recommend that woollen garments should be moth-proofed? If so do you advise home or expert treatment?

It is an excellent plan to have woollen clothes moth-proofed and this applies just as much to woollen woven materials as to hand and machine-knitted garments. Naturally the cleaners are likely to do the job more thoroughly than the housewife because they have the necessary equipment, backed by long experience. But the housewife can buy liquids to spray in cupboards and drawers and wardrobes to discourage moths; it can also be used on upholstery, curtains and carpets. "Rentokil" Mothproofer is one that I have used with success.

Is it possible to have clothes retextured successfully when they have been worn and are a little thin in parts? If so, who will do it?

Providing the material is still strong it can be retextured successfully, and it is up to you to choose just how much more "body" you want in the material. Your cleaners will advise you on this and also do the job for you.

How can evening shoes be cleaned?

Gilt and silver kid shoes can be cleaned with the merest trace of soapy water on a piece of cotton wool. Special gold and silver creams are available for recoating the leather.

Can long white kid evening gloves be cleaned at home?

It is inadvisable because they shrink when wetted and become hard if cleaned with the usual grease solvents. Send them to the cleaners.

I have a piece of very nice hat veiling I want to stiffen; what should I use?

Gum arabic is excellent for this job. Put 2 oz. gum arabic in a jar containing $\frac{1}{2}$ pint of water; stand this in a pan of water and heat until the gum is dissolved then strain and bottle. Use about 2 to 3 teaspoonsful to $\frac{1}{2}$ pint of water, rinse in this mixture and iron damp.

How can I clean a plastic handbag?

Rub over with a soft cloth wrung out in soap and water then dry with a clean cloth.

My suède belt has gone very greasy and shiny. Can I revive it?

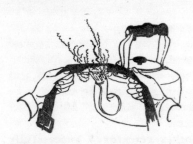

Rub over with a grease solvent like carbon tetrachloride then when dry steam the belt over the spout of a kettle of boiling water. Rub any remaining shiny parts with very fine sandpaper and apply suède cleaner in the usual way; when dry rub up with a wire or rubber brush.

Is there any way of removing tarnish from silver lamé?

Make a thin paste of powdered magnesia and carbon tetrachloride and apply this to the lamé. Leave to dry then brush off, using a fairly stiff brush. This will not remove all the tarnish but it should help considerably to improve the appearance. Store in blue tissue paper to prevent further tarnishing.

Whenever I wash my "washable" leather gloves they come out very hard in spite of all precautions.

The gloves must be made of rather a hard leather. Boil up an ounce of glycerine or olive oil with a cupful of soap suds and add these to the soapy washing water—they should help considerably to keep the leather pliable.

PESTS

I wish I could manage to keep the house clear of flies in hot weather. Can you advise me?

It is, of course, impossible to prevent flies coming into the house unless you keep the doors and windows tightly closed or netted, but you can do a lot to help to get rid of them. From the Pest Infestation Laboratory, Slough, I received the following advice:

First, see that the flies are not tempted to set up home in your dustbin; they love to breed in fish-heads, bones and wet refuse, so burn these whenever possible. If you *must* put them into the bin wrap them carefully in newspaper and replace the bin lid tightly.

Indoors, you can paint a solution of 5 per cent. D.D.T. in refined kerosene over window ledges, picture rails, and other places where flies are seen to land often. This method is slow acting but very effective and economical, leaves no stain and should rid the room of flies overnight.

For a sudden influx of flies in warm weather use an aerosol—one or two light sprays are sufficient to clear a room of flies; cover all food and utensils while you are spraying the aerosol and for at least ten minutes after because the liquid hangs in the air for some time.

How can I get rid of black beetles in my kitchen?

Beetles like warmth and darkness, so pay particular attention to dark, warm corners of the kitchen. Fill all cracks with a plastic wood filler, or, in the case of plaster, with a preparation such as

"Alabastine". Sprinkle D.D.T., or better still, a mixture of D.D.T. and pyrethrum powder, in the favourite haunts every night, paying extra attention to corners and crevices. If pyrethrum is used the powder must be carefully cleaned away each morning before domestic animals or children are about because it is poisonous. Cover all food carefully at night against the beetles.

How can you prevent earwigs coming indoors during the summer?

Cut down creeping plants on walls that would enable earwigs to enter the house easily through the windows and sprinkle paradichlorbenzene in nooks and crannies on windowsills, and round doors, etc.

Our house has been invaded by ants. What should we do?

Cover all sweet foods carefully and remove them from the low

shelves; if the ants are very numerous stand the sweet foods on a table or sideboard with the legs resting in bowls of cold water to prevent the ants reaching the food.

D.D.T. preparations and other ant destroyers are available but the only lasting cure is to destroy the nest, which is usually out of doors, with a proprietary preparation or by pouring boiling water into the nest.

Every autumn we get occasional field mice in the house and we believe they get in through the ventilation gratings. But it seems unwise to block these up.

Cover the gratings with very fine wire mesh sold for the job and pay special attention to damaged gratings.

Our district has recently been plagued by rats and it

seems useless for one or two residents to combat the plague while the remainder will not be bothered to take action. What do you suggest?

This is quite clearly a job for a professional rat-catcher. You can usually obtain his services free of charge through the local Health Authority, generally to be found at the Town Hall or County Council offices.

Mosquitoes and gnats breed in our rainwater butt, and are becoming a real nuisance. Is there any cure other than emptying the rainwater butt, which I do not want to do?

You need not empty the rainwater butt. Just put a tablespoonful of ordinary paraffin oil on to the surface and the mosquitoes and gnats will not worry you again.

Our upholstered furniture has got moth in it. How should I treat it?

Clean thoroughly with a vacuum cleaner then spray it well with a good insecticide. Repeat this treatment at regular intervals all through the summer.

Is there any way of getting rid of moth in a carpet?

Clean thoroughly with a vacuum cleaner, take up the carpet, and hang over a line out of doors in sunlight for several hours. Do the same with the underfelt, and scrub the boards very well with hot soapy water containing carbolic disinfectant. Put back the underlay and carpet, when the boards are dry, and spray each very thoroughly with insecticide. Spray regularly throughout the summer.

One corner of my carpet has been attacked by moth. This corner is beneath the settee. How can I treat it?

Damp a thick rough towel and lay over the corner of the carpet.

Press with a very hot iron till the towel is quite dry. The steam that results from this treatment helps to destroy both the moth eggs and maggots. Repeat as often as necessary till no sign of moth remains. For extra precaution, spray with insecticide.

There are definite signs of bookworm in several old books that we have. We are loath to part with them; is there a cure?

Yes! But do isolate them at once because the worm can spread to other books. Place the books in a closed tin with a piece of cotton wool soaked in ether or ethylene dichloride, and seal the tin with sticky tape. Leave for 24 hours then take out the books and leave in the open air for the fumes to clear away. Repeat this treatment four or five times at intervals of about two weeks so that you destroy any eggs that may hatch out.